Angela Carter

Twayne's English Authors Series

Kinley Roby, Editor

TEAS 540

ANGELA CARTER
Photograph by Miriam Berkley

Angela Carter

Alison Lee

University of Western Ontario

Twayne Publishers
An Imprint of Simon & Schuster Macmillan
New York

Prentice Hall International
London • Mexico City • New Delhi • Singapore • Sydney • Toronto

Twayne's English Authors Series No. 540

Angela Carter
Alison Lee

Twayne Publishers
1633 Broadway
New York, NY 10019

Library of Congress Cataloging-in-Publication Data
Lee, Alison, 1957–
     Angela Carter / Alison Lee.
          p.   cm.   — (Twayne's English authors series ; TEAS 540)
     ISBN 0-8057-7823-3 (alk. paper)
     1. Carter, Angela, 1940–   —Criticism and interpretation.
     2. Women and literature—England—History—20th century.   I. Title.
     II. Series.
     PR6053.A73Z75   1997
     823'.914—dc21   96-39867
                                                                              CIP

10 9 8 7 6 5 4 3 2

Printed in the United States of America

For Ernie and Sarah

Contents

Preface

"I am known in my circle," Carter writes in *Expletives Deleted*, "as notoriously foul-mouthed. It's a familiar paradox—the soft-spoken, middle-aged English gentlewoman who swears like a trooper when roused."[1] When Carter died in February 1992, friends and fellow writers expressed their grief in an outpouring of encomiums for a writer and a woman who died too soon. Her friend Lorna Sage, who has made an extensive contribution to critical material on Carter's work, writes that "her life as a writer, and so much of the life *in* her writing, was intransigent, bloody-minded, mocking, self-conscious and excessive."[2] Although, as Sage points out, Carter has now become "alarmingly 'central,' "[3] she had been, for a long time, hard to place. Her novels and short fictions are romances, adventures, fairy stories, science fictions, and Gothic tales. They are evidence of a keen intellect, a feminist consciousness, and a polemical cast of mind. Her fiction and nonfiction alike indicate that she had a passionate belief in the power of language and literature to instruct as well as to delight, and she never divorced her literary practice from her political concerns. Her writing is complex, difficult, and didactic, as well as witty, delightful, and exuberant.

Several threads weave in and out of Carter's works, although her novels are remarkable for their originality in plot and character. One consistent interest is the position of women in literature, in history, and in the world, and her corpus provides a large number of perspectives from which to see women and from which women may see themselves. From the masochism of her early characters to the strong self-sufficiency of her later ones, Carter's female characters are victims and victors. They are mothers, dancers, aerialists, technological inventions, objects of desire, and above all, they are capable of feeling and expressing erotic pleasure. Carter's female characters never exist purely within the realm of her stories; her range of literary references is broad, sometimes overwhelming, but each of her characters is placed within a tradition of Western literary culture. By the time of *Wise Children* (1991), her female characters are themselves writing back to this tradition and deciding just how they are going to place themselves within it. In some cases, I have selected items from Carter's literary background for specific discussion, but for the most part, I have simply referred to them as creating a multitude of voices against and within which to read Carter's works. Despite her very clear stance on certain issues, Carter pays her reader the compliment of intelligence. She assumes a reader who would be able to respond in a variety of ways to her fiction. To list the other fictions to which she refers would not only be an impossible task but also deny readers the joy of making their own discoveries.

It has sometimes been difficult for feminist critics to embrace Carter wholeheartedly. Not all of her representations of women are emancipatory, but this reservation on the part of some critics has to be balanced against the extraordinary complexity with which Carter viewed relations between men and women. She called herself a feminist, but her feminism is no more monolithic than her representations of female sexuality. As is clear from her fairy tales, women can not only run with wolves but be wolves and even seduce wolves. The possibilities are endless, although some of them are not universally attractive. For me, this diversity is what makes Carter's work so appealing. She *is* bloody-minded, often literally so, and her characters' eroticism takes many forms, some of them pornographic and downright bestial. Her voice, however, is consistently ironic, and she is suspicious of anything that presents itself as a universal answer to any question. This skepticism is what aligns her with postmodernism.

Postmodern novels of the British school are often distinguished by their historic content. They return to a moment of history and imaginatively fill in the gaps left by official histories, gaps such as domestic lives, particularly those of women and other characters marginalized by the people who record world events. *Wise Children* and *Nights at the Circus*, for example, show the history of the past 100 years from the perspective of bawdy and irreverent entertainers such as dance hall girls and circus performers. Theirs are the "other" perspectives, which are just as important as, but excluded by, official histories. Even when Carter's novels are set in the future or an unspecified time, though, the historical perspective is maintained by a literary history that has been equally important in shaping how we view the world. Carter's novels often play with genre, as well as with specific literary works. Her novels use the picaresque, fairy-tale, realist, Gothic, and other genres, some of which have either excluded women characters from major roles or have created women characters who are helpless and in need of rescue. While assuming that her readers will recognize the conventions of these genres, Carter undermines and reworks them.

The result of Carter's mixing of genres, her remarkably broad-ranging references to other novels and cultural icons, and her postmodern skepticism, gender bending, and even species switching is a real delight in the power of language to captivate and transform. There are always a number of voices speaking in Carter's novels, and although every reading hears some of them, others are still murmuring and shouting in the background. Most important, however, is the voice of the woman writer and how she converses with, and finds her own language in, the face of a Western literary tradition of largely male voices. Carter is not a separatist; she does not want to deny or exclude the canon of male writers, but she does want to have a good, solid argument with them. Her feminism and postmodernism combine as she takes the literary tradition and its representations of women, uses and abuses them, and tries to create other representations in response.

In this book, I have focused on Carter's novels, some of which have had less critical attention than her short fiction. When the novels have received a good deal of such attention, as in the case of *Nights at the Circus*, for example, I have tried to find other themes and arguments than those in already-published material. Carter's imagination is prolific, and the differences among her novels are perhaps more significant than their similarities. In examining each novel, I have commented on her treatments of women, and these are as various and complex as the novels themselves. I have also woven Carter's nonfictional voice into several of the analyses, not to raise the critical conundrum of "intentionality," but to include, as one possible reading, her own thoughts on her work. Because her own views on literature and politics have much to do with her literary representations, it is interesting to read the fictional and nonfictional voices together. In reading all of her voices, I came more and more to like and admire Angela Carter as a person and a writer who had convictions she was not afraid to express. Salman Rushdie captures the delight of both writing and writer in his introduction to her collected short stories, *Burning Your Boats*, as "by turns formal and outrageous, exotic and demotic, exquisite and coarse, precious and raunchy, fabulist and socialist, purple and black. Her novels are like nobody else's."[4]

Chronology

1940   Angela Olive Stalker born May 7 in Eastbourne, Sussex, to which her mother and brother had been evacuated during the war. Spends the war with her maternal grandmother in South Yorkshire.

1960   Marries Paul Carter, moves to Bristol.

1962–1965   Reads English at Bristol University, specializing in medieval literature.

1966   First novel, *Shadow Dance*, published.

1967   *The Magic Toyshop* published; wins John Llewellyn Rhys Memorial Prize.

1968   *Several Perceptions* published; wins Somerset Maugham Award.

1969   *Heroes and Villains*.

1969–1972   Lives and works in Japan.

1971   *Love*.

1972   Divorces Paul Carter; publishes *The Infernal Desire Machines of Doctor Hoffman*.

1973–1976   Lives in Bath Spa.

1974   *Fireworks*, first collection of short stories, published.

1975   Begins to write regularly for *New Society*.

1976–1978   Fellow in creative writing at Sheffield University.

1977   Moves to South London with Mark Pearce; serves on the advisory board of Virago Publishers; publishes *The Passion of New Eve*.

1979   *The Bloody Chamber* wins the Cheltenham Festival of Literature Award; *The Sadeian Woman: An Exercise in Cultural History*, commissioned by Virago Press.

1980–1981   Visiting Professor in the Writing Program at Brown University, Providence, Rhode Island.

1982   Publishes *Nothing Sacred*, a collection of her journalism.

1983   Son Alexander Pearce born.

1984–1987   Teaches part-time at the University of East Anglia.

1984   Publishes *Nights at the Circus*; writer in residence, University of Adelaide, South Australia; *The Company of Wolves* (based on the story of the same name in *The Bloody Chamber*), directed by Neil Jordan, released on film.

1985   *Nights at the Circus* is the joint winner of the James Tait Black Memorial Prize; *Black Venus* and *Come unto These Yellow Sands: Four Radio Plays* published. Carter teaches in Austin, Texas.

1986   Teaches in Iowa City, Iowa.

1987   Film of *The Magic Toyshop*, directed by David Wheatly, released.

1988   Teaches in Albany, New York.

1990   Publishes *The Virago Book of Fairy Tales*, the first of two edited collections, the second of which is published in 1992.

1991   Publishes *Wise Children*.

1992   Dies February 16 of cancer.

Chapter One
A Sketch of Angela Carter

I am the pure product of an advanced, industrialised, post-imperialist country in decline.[1]

Angela Carter's literary executor, Susannah Clapp, writes that Carter always traveled with a sketch pad and that drawings and paintings spilled from the drawers in her study.[2] Carter's writing invokes such a sense of the visual in both imagery and description that it is not surprising she should have been interested in various modes of capturing how and what she saw. She was a prolific writer in many genres, and although she is best known for her novels and short stories, she also wrote radio, screen, and stage plays as well as poetry, stories for children, journalism, and an opera libretto. She translated the fairy tales of Charles Perrault, edited two collections of fairy tales and an anthology of subversive stories by women, and wrote a polemical book on the Marquis de Sade. That she also had a talent for drawing adds one more achievement to an already remarkable list. She loved to teach and was invited to do so as writer-in-residence in Britain, the United States, and Australia. Her publisher at Chatto and Windus, Carmen Callil, calls Carter "the Johnny Appleseed of English literature: all over the English-speaking world are incendiary bombs planted by Angela."[3] Among Carter's students were Glenn Patterson, Kazuo Ishiguro, and Pat Barker. Despite all of this, her writing was not as well known during her life as it became after her death. Although she served as a judge for Britain's prestigious Booker Prize, she never won it. Virago Press, which had republished many of her novels, sold out of them shortly after her death, and since then she has become one of the most studied contemporary writers in Britain.

The most sustained narrative of Carter's life appears in Lorna Sage's *Angela Carter*. This brief literary biography, as well as anecdotal information conveyed in obituaries, and Carter's own reminiscences create a kind of patchwork of the events in her life. Given the amount of material she wrote, it is tempting to wonder how she found the time to do much else, particularly because she also had a son, a family life, and many, many friends. Her essays about growing up during and after World War II appear in *Nothing Sacred*, and she wrote an affectionate portrait of her father called "Sugar Daddy." These pieces share something of the tone of her fiction. As Sage comments, Carter refused "to observe any decorous distinction between art and life, so that she was inventive in reality as well as in creating plots and characters for her books."[4] Her journalism, samples of which are collected in *Nothing Sacred* and *Expletives Deleted*, is spiced with personal comments, and the enthusiastic "trainspotter" of Carter's writing will notice that some of the details of her private life also appear in her novels and short stories. The known facts of her life do little to capture its complexity. She was not, however, shy about expressing her thoughts, and her views of the world come through most clearly in her prose.

There are discrepancies in the dictionary entries and obituaries about some of the events in Carter's life: her age when she died, the date of her son's birth, and even the spelling of her second husband's name. We cannot, of course, know whether such inconsistencies would have appealed to her inventive imagination or infuriated her by their shabbiness. Her friends, however, in their affectionate anecdotes, do not disagree about her wisdom, her loyalty, or her wicked sense of humor. Robert Coover writes that Carter's telephone voice was "a reed instrument of marvelous versatility and emotional range, chimelike in its bold ringing of metaphors, saturated with wry, self-deprecating humor, and utterly compelling."[5] Carmen Callil called Carter "the oracle we all consulted."[6] Salman Rushdie relates the story of their last visit, at which Carter was "courteous enough to overcome mortal suffering for the gentility of a formal afternoon tea."[7] Almost all Carter's friends mention her perceptiveness, her particular talent for looking at things carefully. In his "A Passionate Remembrance," Coover describes this talent most touchingly: "And if she clearly saw through everything and everyone else, she surely saw through you as well, and if she did so and loved you still and with such faithfulness, how could you help but feel in some way spectacularly chosen?"[8]

In much of Carter's writing about herself there is a mixture of certainty and tentativeness. Along with the confident originality that characterizes her journalism is a repeated trope of expressing her sense that she was an outsider or a foreigner. This appears not only in her writing about Japan, where she spent two years in the early 1970s, or in her comments about visits to the United States, but also in the description of her father's Scottish village and of parts of her native London. Sage suggests that Carter cultivated "the viewpoint of an alien in order to defamiliarize the landscape of habit" (Sage, *Angela Carter*, 2). Carter writes in *Nothing Sacred* that her failure to learn Japanese while she was living in Japan resulted in her "trying to understand things by simply looking at them very, very carefully."[9] Both comments imply that Carter's willing estrangement is an important key to her perspective. In her journalism, Carter's "alien" viewpoint does indeed defamiliarize the familiar cultural artifacts she explores, and it encourages her readers to look at ordinary things in unusual ways. In her fiction, Carter creates picaresque protagonists who see the world around them with strangers' eyes. Even when her novels seem to be at their most opaque, it is worth remembering that their aim is to jar readers out of the "landscape of habit" and into a habit of very careful looking.

Angela Olive Stalker was born on May 7, 1940, in Eastbourne, England, to Olive (Farthing) Stalker and Hugh Alexander Stalker. With what Carter called "the family talent for magic realism" (*NS*, 4), her mother once told her that she confirmed her pregnancy on the very day World War II was declared. Carter was born the week Dunkirk fell; Eastbourne seeming too close to Hitler's armies across the Channel, her mother, brother, and grandmother repaired to South Yorkshire, whence her mother's family originally hailed. Carter's reminiscences of the war years center on her maternal grandmother, who "talked broad Yorkshire," "hated tears and whining" (*NS*, 11), and reared her granddaughter as a "tough, arrogant and pragmatic Yorkshire child" (*NS*, 4).

After the war, the family returned to Balham, South London, where Carter went to school. As an adolescent, she was anorexic, a condition she attributed to being "ludicrously overprotected": "my parent's concern to protect me from predatory boys was only equalled by the enthusiasm with which the boys I did occasionally meet protected themselves against me."[10] Yet the picture she paints of her family life is generally affectionate, and her depiction of her childhood home highlights its dreamlike aura: "life passed at a languorous pace, everything was gently untidy, and none of the clocks ever told the right time" (*NS*, 14). She writes with particular warmth of her father, a journalist, who was in his mid-forties when Carter was born, and moved back to his family home in Scotland when Carter's mother died. Carter describes him as handsome, sentimental, and volatile, and relates his special relationship with cats, flotillas of which would follow him home from his job on the night news desk. He was less sympathetic to her boyfriends; on a visit to Scotland, Carter recalls, she and Mark had to sleep in separate rooms, and in

lieu of the legendary sword, her father electrified Mark's bed by plug-
ging its metal base into the electric light fixture: "Mark noticed how the
bed throbbed when he put his hand on it and disconnected every plug in
sight. We ate breakfast, next morning, as if nothing untoward had happened, and I should say, in the context of my father's house, it had
not."[11]

After her marriage to Paul Carter in 1960, she and her husband
moved to Bristol where, in 1965, Carter took a degree in English from
Bristol University. During a summer vacation, she wrote *Shadow Dance*
(1966). Two more novels were quickly to follow: *The Magic Toyshop*
(1967), which won the John Llewellen Rhys Memorial Prize, and *Several
Perceptions* (1968), for which Carter received the Somerset Maugham
Award. Having separated from her husband (her divorce was finalized in
1972), she used the £500 in prize money to travel to Japan. Carter lived
in Japan for two years, "making a living one way and another" (*NS*, 28),
because she wanted to see what it was like to live in a culture that had
never been Judeo-Christian. In Japan, she wrote, "I learned what it is to
be a woman and became radicalised" (*NS*, 28).

As Sage describes it, Carter's return to England was difficult because
she had to reestablish her place in the literary community. Although she
wrote for *New Society* and the *Guardian* and had an Arts Council fellow-
ship from 1976 to 1978 in Sheffield, where she moved after living for
three years in Bath, she suffered, as Sage puts it, "a thin time" (Sage,
Angela Carter, 31). Despite Carter's prolific output during the decade,
she had no secure relationship with a publisher. *The Infernal Desire
Machines of Doctor Hoffman*, begun in Japan and published in 1972, was
largely ignored by critics. *Fireworks* was published in 1974, *The Passion of
New Eve* and the translation of *The Fairy Tales of Charles Perrault* in 1977,
and *The Bloody Chamber* and *The Sadeian Woman* in 1979. The latter had
been commissioned by the then-fledgling Virago Press, on whose editorial board Carter also served, although, as Carmen Callil notes, " 'Commission' . . . is the wrong word to use—she wrote what she wanted
to."[12] Sage quotes a letter from this time in which Carter refers to
Virago's plan to publish and republish the works of women writers. The
tenor of the letter strikes me as vintage Carter: "I suppose I am moved
towards it by the desire that no daughter of mine should ever be in a
position to be able to write: BY GRAND CENTRAL STATION I SAT DOWN
AND WEPT, exquisite prose though it might contain. (BY GRAND CENTRAL
STATION I TORE OFF HIS BALLS would be more like it I should hope)"
(Sage, *Angela Carter*, 32).

In the late 1970s, Carter settled with Mark Pearce in Clapham, South London. Chatto and Windus became her publisher in 1982 when Carmen Callil moved there from Virago. In 1984 Carter was to publish *Nights at the Circus*, the novel for which she is best known, which won the James Tait Black Memorial Prize. While writing *Nights at the Circus*, Carter became pregnant; in November 1983, when she was 43, her son Alexander Pearce was born.

Carter's final novel, *Wise Children*, was, as she said in an interview, her favorite.[13] It is perhaps too easy to view the novel with hindsight as a swan song, dealing as it does with issues of personal history, public culture, birth, aging, and death. Published in 1991, the novel appeared too near her death to avoid such speculation. It is not that these concerns were new to Carter's writing; rather, there is a poignancy to their appearance in her last novel. However, *Wise Children* is too raucous and too joyful for any sort of maudlin interpretation, and in that subversive sense, it is an appropriate swan song. "A good writer," Carter wrote, "can make you believe time stands still,"[14] and the legacy of *Wise Children* is that time is best spent with laughter and optimism.

In 1991, Carter discovered she had lung cancer. She died in her own bed on February 16, 1992. Robert Coover writes that she "met her final illness with this characteristic mix of comic sorrow, rueful comedy, studying her illness as though it were another metaphor to be wrestled with."[15] In the introduction to Carter's posthumous collection of short stories, *American Ghosts and Old World Wonders*, Susannah Clapp recalls that Carter's directions to those dealing with her literary estate were expansive. To make money for her husband, Mark, and her son, Alexander, "any one of her fifteen books could be set to music or acted on ice."[16] The Ice Capades would never be the same.

Chapter Two

Carter's Themes, Style, and Other Writing

Angela Carter is the child who sees that the emperor has no clothes. She has a heretical imagination, and she leaves not a single emperor in any doubt as to his nakedness. Her virtuoso writing style is often so extravagant that it rouses critics to similar heights in trying to describe it. Because her fiction combines so many genres, conventions, and styles, it is hard to say with any confidence that it fits into a particular area of literary study. This catholicity, together with her views on sexuality, her idiosyncratic reading of the Marquis de Sade, and her celebration of women's eroticism, makes Carter's oeuvre one of the most compelling in contemporary British writing. Margaret Atwood calls Carter's short fiction a "plum pudding," although this sense of rich delight is a rather accurate metaphor for her longer fiction as well.[1] Mind you, one is almost as likely to pull a shard of glass out of this pudding as a plum; Carter is never one to let her reader simply consume her fiction with a self-satisfied sigh. One has to be alert and prepared for surprises. The prudish or the easily shocked should beware; as Atwood cleverly notes, Carter's fiction often delves into the macabre: "Not for her Hemingway's clean, well-lighted place, or Orwell's clear prose like a pane of glass. She prefers instead a dirty, badly-lit place, with gnawed bones in the corner and dusty mirrors you'd best not consult."[2] There is also much that is witty and wise; fiction and nonfiction alike look askance at those parts of our literary and popular culture whose symbols may be hiding something coercive, dangerous, or downright silly.

Carter is an extraordinary reader of all forms of culture and has a keen sense of the absurd. In her journalism, she leaves no sacred cow unskewered. In D. H. Lawrence's *Women in Love*, for example, she follows the trail of Gudrun's stockings to reveal Lawrence's fetishistic obsession with women's clothes and to dispute the accepted wisdom that he has an insider's sympathy for a woman's needs: "(How could they have afforded to dress like that on teachers' salaries in those days?) It is the detail of the 'linen lace' that gives Lawrence away, of course. He is a true *aficionado* of furbelows. What the hell is linen lace? I'm sure I don't know" (*NS*, 163). Of *Gone with the Wind*, starring "Clark 'Jug Ears' Gable" and Vivien Leigh as an "anorexic, over-dressed Scarlett O'Hara" (*NS*, 140), Carter writes, "But goodness me, how enjoyable it is! I curled up in my armchair, giggling helplessly, weakly muttering: 'Break his kneecaps,' about every five minutes, sometimes more often" (*NS*, 141). It is impossible, having read her pointed insights, to think the same way about any object of her critique. From pornography to mainstream art, from family romances to cultural difference, Carter probes the hidden reality behind the image and reveals that reality with stroke of her acerbic pen.

The Sadeian Woman

The Sadeian Woman is the most controversial of all Carter's cultural critiques. Its mode of inquiry is not unlike her journalism, but in trying to suggest ways in which the Marquis de Sade might be important to women, the stakes are rather higher. Appearing at almost the midpoint in her literary career, *The Sadeian Woman* contains themes and ideas that had obviously concerned Carter before the book's publication and continued to do so afterward. Sexual cruelty, of course, is not uncommon in Carter's fiction. In her first novel, *Shadow Dance*, Ghislaine is brutally disfigured by her lover and then later in the novel begs for even more pain and humiliation. In Carter's last novel, *Wise Children*, Tiffany is abandoned by her lover, Tristram, when she discovers she is pregnant. *Wise Children* is a comedy, but there is nothing comic about Tiffany's appearance on Tristram's live television show wearing only a football sweater and underwear, her feet bleeding from a long walk in stiletto heels. Her humiliation at Tristram's hands is repeated here in front of a live audience, and the spectacle of her misery is tragic. All does end more or less happily, but Tiffany is still pregnant, and Tristram manages to hide his cruelty behind a whining disclaimer that he is not ready to be a father. Between these two novels are others in which women characters are raped, abandoned because they have been impregnated, captured, prostituted, and humiliated.

To suggest that all of this makes Carter herself a Sadeian woman, however, is to misread the manner in which she represents these events. Certainly, she is interested in the workings of power as they are manifested in sexual relations, and in this she has something in common with Sade, although she would hardly agree with his methods. For Sade, the gratification of sexual desire is entirely bound up with power. While he questions the status quo by showing the corruption inherent in those systems that profit from power—the clergy, the law, and the government—he nonetheless celebrates the absolute power of the strong over the weak and of the rich over the poor. His writing is anarchic, but his is the anarchy of the Reign of Terror. Sade's logic is often tenuous, but the point of his philosophy is that nature neither rewards virtue nor punishes vice, but creates the weak and the strong with the intention that the first should always be subordinate to the second. Although civil law may try to establish an order based on virtue, civil law can never prevail against the laws of nature. Libertarian individualism requires that the weak be at the mercy of the strong, a relationship that Sade almost always puts in economic terms. To imitate the Sadeian libertines is to follow the laws of nature, and therefore to eschew responsibility for individual action. Vice wins over virtue, not because vice is rewarded by fate but because the person who practices vice has taken control of his or her fortunes.

Carter does not doubt that Sade is pornographic, and she is not trying to save him for future generations by protesting his liberation of sexuality from cultural restraints. In the introduction, she describes her book as a "late-twentieth-century interpretation of some of the problems he raises about the culturally determined nature of women and of the relations between men and women that result from it."[3] Perhaps one of the reasons she finds Sade so compelling is that some of his views on sexuality crop up in twentieth-century culture under the guise of sexual liberation. She ruthlessly satirizes two particular examples in her essays in *Nothing Sacred* on *Playgirl* and *Inside Linda Lovelace*, both of which trumpet themselves as examples of women's sexual emancipation. In "Lovely Linda," Carter suggests that the notion of permissiveness is nothing but a ruse: "who is it that permits me? Why the self same institutions that hitherto forbade me!" (*NS*, 147). Lovelace celebrates her sexual freedom without any notion of "social or spiritual emancipation" (*NS*, 147), but rather on the basis of a misguided idea that she herself is free. From Carter's reading, it seems clear that Lovelace's sexual acrobatics make her a successful film star because nothing in them challenges the spectators' attitudes. Reducing her sexual activity to an abstraction, Lovelace willingly replicates, in spirit if not in kind, the sort of subjugation in which Sade's libertines revel. Pornography for Carter can be subversive only when it "begins to comment on real relations in the real world" (*SW*, 19); all Lovelace succeeds in doing is to relegate those relations to a "geometric intersection of parts" (*NS*, 149).

A similar, though more complex, critique is aimed at *Playgirl*, from whose editorial philosophy Carter quotes a typically Sadeian line: "the success of individual liberation is the quintessence of our survival" (*NS*, 101–2). One achieves this liberation, suggest the magazine's ads, by bowing down before accepted stereotypes. Whereas *Playgirl*'s nudes are associated by their biographies and poses with money and power, and the female reader is to be seduced by their protestations of love and romance, Carter's recapitulation of the history of the male and female nude in art adds another dimension to the display. Despite the history of depersonalization in portraying the female nude, Carter points out that a woman naked "can never be less than herself for her value in the world resides more in her skin than in her clothes" (*NS*, 103). There is a different vocabulary of expressions and gestures "available for women in relation to men that does not exist for men in relation to women" (*NS*, 104), and so whereas the female nude has historically displayed her body as a site of both nourishment and sexuality, the male nude has no such iconography to draw on. Carter discovers some representation of the male body for male pleasure but, disturbingly, finds repeatedly "the icon of the naked man in physical torment" (*NS*, 104). The pornography of the male nude, she argues, is a supreme form of sadomasochism, and *Playgirl*'s failure to titillate is because the kitsch bodies on display have absolutely nothing to do with "two millenia of St. Sebastian transfixed by arrows, St. Lawrence with his gridiron, St. Bartholomew being flayed" (*NS*, 105). Here sexual liberation meets the history of torture, reminding readers that the "porno-kitsch" (*NS*, 103) of *Playgirl*, as Carter calls it, must be seen in the historical mirror of flayed flesh.

None of her arguments about pornography in the above guises is, however, quite as controversial as her suggestion in *The Sadeian Woman* that pornography can have a place in the service of women. As in most of Carter's cultural criticism, her point in the "Polemical Preface" is deceptively simple, or at least it seems simple once it has been articulated as clearly as this. Primarily, her argument develops from the idea that sexual relations mirror social ones, a notion that explains to some extent the nature of sexual behavior in her novels. "Flesh," Carter writes, "comes to us out of history" (*SW*, 10), as do the mechanisms that repress and permit both sex and sexual attraction. Class, race, religion, education, and gender all have an effect upon choice of partner and manner of sexual expression, and therefore the "notion of a universality of human experience is a confidence trick" (*SW*, 12). In the opening pages of her preface, she argues vehemently that the most private and intimate of human experiences is governed by ideology. "We do not go to bed in simple pairs" (*SW*, 9); rather, we take all of our familial, social, and cultural histories with us. Carter makes this point forcefully because her complaint about pornography is that it denies these very real facts of social existence by reducing sex to the level of graffiti scribblings, "the probe and the fringed hole" (*SW*, 4). By doing so, pornography creates sex as an abstraction and ascribes to it the false universality of myth.

Carter's essays on *Playgirl* and Linda Lovelace's biography very specifically attack their lack of historical consciousness and try to reestablish some form of context for their representations of the male and female body. In *The Sadeian Woman*, Carter puts this same notion in more theoretical terms. Pornography maintains the status quo precisely because pornography creates images of sexuality in a vacuum, thereby diffusing its subversive potential. Carter speculates that the more pornography acquires literary techniques, "the more deeply subversive it is likely to be in that the more likely it is to affect real relations in the real world" (*SW*, 19). Were it to do so, then it might have the potential to change the nature of sexual, and therefore social, relations between men and women. The "moral pornographer" (*SW*, 19) would reinvest pornography with all of the contextual issues that Carter sees as lacking, and this would make it women's ally.

The moral pornographer is to become a "terrorist of the imagination" (*SW*, 21) because he or she will present sexual cruelties and acts of violence in such a way as to rid them of eroticism. Sade, Carter contends, is just such a terrorist because his descriptions of sexuality tie such acts most clearly to the workings of a corrupt and unfree society. What Carter finds attractive in Sade, then, would seem to be his honesty, as well as the representations that free women's sexuality from a purely reproductive function. If sex is power in Sade, then women too can have that power. Although these aspects are appealing, Carter is neither reading Sade as a protofeminist nor condemning him outright. This, after all, is a *polemical* preface. She does not doubt his misogyny, but she praises his revealing the social conditions that give rise to misogyny.

From this perspective, it is useful to speculate whether Carter saw her own novels as fulfilling the demands of a moral pornography. Although she is against pornography in the kitsch sense exhibited by *Playgirl* and Linda Lovelace, Carter's own writing does contain sexual cruelties that might be described as pornographic, and she has been described by one critic as "the high priestess of post-graduate porn."[4] In her early novels, particularly *Shadow Dance*, the violence against women is sadistic,

despite the clear definition of the conditions that perpetrate such violence. Ghislaine responds to violence by embracing the role of victim
that has been thrust upon her, and the tragedy is offset only slightly by
Emily's saving herself. In *Love,* Annabel commits suicide because it is the
only way she can assert a will of her own. Within her own terms, if
Carter imaginatively represents the circumstances of oppression in all its
ugliness and brutality, she does so from an ethical position. Carter has
been criticized for creating her characters from within an iconography of
domination and submission, and thus not imagining a different kind of
erotic representation but only a response to its traditional formulation.
Whether one accepts this critique as valid has much to do with what
one sees as the function of literature. Carter writes that if nobody
"acknowledges art as a means of *knowing* the world, then art is relegated
to a kind of rumpus room of the mind and the irresponsibility of the
artist and the irrelevance of art to actual living becomes part and parcel
of the practice of art" (*SW,* 13). Carter sees her own responsibility as
directed toward raising the issues and pointing out their relevance, and
her aim is to heighten awareness and encourage change; but the reader
also has a responsibility. Reading Carter's works is always an active
process, and this equal exchange between reader and text finally allows
new formulations to arise from the old.

Postmodernism

Postmodern Conventions

Although I have used the term sparingly, postmodernism underlies
much of my reading of Carter because I see her skepticism and her challenge to orthodoxy as very much within postmodernism's parameters.
The danger of using the term is that by itself it has provoked enormous
hostility toward, and some nasty criticism of, those who are considered
to be practitioners. Shortly after Carter's death, for example, John Bayley wrote a peculiarly backhanded "appreciation" of her work, in which
he lists several characteristics Carter shares with postmodernism. Both,
according to Bayley, are militantly orthodox, dated, fashionable, permis-
sive, and politically correct; indeed, "whatever spirited arabesques and
feats of descriptive imagination Carter may perform, she always comes
to rest in the right ideological position."[5] Hermione Lee has taken Bayley to task for his comments, and one of her observations is that "if you
now want to dismiss a feminist author, you can make her sound rigid

and intolerant by giving her the 'PC' label."[6] It is really hard to imagine Carter coming to rest in any one ideological position, although she was indeed intolerant of some things. Her nonfiction in particular suggests that she did not suffer fools gladly. She *is* a feminist author, and she does criticize institutions, including literary ones, that have been particularly doctrinaire in their representations of women. She holds these institutions up for piercing scrutiny, raucous laughter, and crusty cynicism. These characteristics of her writing place her within a literary postmodernism that has little to do with Bayley's interpretation.

Without tracing the history of postmodernism, about which much has been written, I am going to discuss those conventions of postmodern fiction that are important to Carter's writing. In many ways, Carter and postmodernism are a splendid match. Contrary to Bayley's characterization, postmodernism is overwhelmingly skeptical, particularly of anything that presents itself as an absolute truth or certainty. Postmodernism is also very much concerned, as Carter's use of it shows, with the ways in which attitudes, beliefs, and myths have come to be regarded as truths. In this sense, postmodernism is concerned with history, not only as a record of past events, but also as the history of literary conventions, genres, and ideas. Linda Hutcheon has coined the term "historiographic metafiction"[7] to describe postmodernism's concern with how we come to know history, as well as with how some fiction exhibits awareness of itself as artifice. In Hutcheon's formulation, postmodernism is inherently paradoxical: "its art forms (and its theory) at once use and abuse, install and then destabilize convention in parodic ways, self-consciously pointing to both their own inherent paradoxes and provisionality and, of course, to their critical or ironic re-reading of the art of the past."[8]

It would be a mistake, however, to assume that postmodern fiction and theory are concerned only with their own processes and those of historical discourse. Indeed, one of the strengths of postmodernism has been its interdisciplinarity, its theoretical and practical drawing on philosophy, science, psychoanalysis, and popular culture. To include the ideas and languages of other disciplines in a fictional context is not to lose the metafictional aspect of fiction, but simply to question whether one discipline is more important than any other. As one would expect from a genre that questions anything that presents itself as an absolute, postmodernism is neither static nor monolithic. While literary postmodernism is primarily concerned with the connections between history and fiction, and with the possibilities for literary narratives, it also takes stock of its interdisciplinarity and edges into politics, an aspect that theorists and critics have been hesitant to address. Postmodernism has always been political in the sense that its attitude of skepticism has always led to questioning and to rethinking, but it has been criticized by some for not being political enough—often for not providing a dogmatic platform to replace the ones it has been tearing down. Postmodernism is *political* because it calls into question the ways in which history has traditionally been recorded, its privileging of some groups and excluding of others, and its claim to objectivity. Fiction for postmodernism cannot be seen as an unproblematic reflection of life, nor as an unproblematic reflection of fiction itself. Postmodernism breaks down hierarchies and reconsiders categories. This challenge to the reader is one of the most exciting aspects of Carter's fiction. Although she is certainly a feminist writer and is intent on tracing and combating social and fictional representations that oppress women, her work questions ideas surrounding such diverse elements as myths of origin, family dynamics, psychoanalysis, sexuality and aggression, performance, popular culture, language, and the literary canon.

Carter is an eminently intellectual writer, and her novels include references to an enormous number of literary, critical, and musical works. She read social and anthropological theories, including the writings of Roland Barthes, Claude Lévi-Strauss, and Michel Foucault, and she was more than conversant with the writings of Sigmund Freud. Ideas from these theorists, as well as writers of fiction, regularly appear in her novels, so that reading them often seems an education in the entire artistic and intellectual store of Western civilization. Carter wrote in the preface to *Come unto These Yellow Sands* that the purpose of narrative for her was to explore ideas, which "is the same thing as telling stories since, for me, a narrative is an argument stated in fictional terms."[9] Although she is seldom doctrinaire, this would imply a clearly didactic aim to her writing. However, she very much wishes to delight as well as to instruct, and she is a consummate entertainer. All manner of performances pervade her work, from the individual character with a flair for dressing up to vaudeville, pantomime, and the circus to film and Shakespeare. Her writing itself is a spectacle. From lush, baroque sentences to wordplay and puns, her language turns as many dizzying somersaults as the winged aerialist in *Nights at the Circus*. Her wit is sometimes wry and ironic, sometimes bawdily funny, and her language evokes equally the opera and pantomime. The bantering tension between her playfulness and her seriousness places her squarely within postmodernism. There is something of the carnival spirit in all her work. In her style as in her intellectual probings, nothing is sacred.

Carter's Postmodern Practice

Carter's writing invokes one of postmodernism's most paradoxical conventions in that it uses the very ideas, genres, and truths that it seeks to criticize. When, for example, she wishes to criticize the genre of realism, as she does in *Several Perceptions*, she writes within the realist genre. When she seeks to change the myths propagated by traditional fairy tales, as in *The Bloody Chamber*, she does so from within the genre itself. Although this strategy is paradoxical, it does show both sides of the story at once. In her use of literary references and allusions, she offers a different context in order to suggest a different way of thinking. This is evident in all her fiction, but perhaps the most obvious example is in her rewritten fairy tales. Historical and literary contexts are important to Carter because her aim is to draw the reader's attention to the way in which those contexts have determined the way we think. Although she may not be able to rely on every reader having an intimate knowledge of specific literary works from the history of Western literature, most readers will be familiar with the conventions of the fairy tale and will be acquainted, for example, with some version of "Little Red Riding Hood" or "Cinderella." Because fairy tales traditionally were tales told rather than written, there are, of course, many different versions of each tale from many different cultures. For every version we read or hear, others are jostling in the background, suggesting diverse readings of the same elements. It is easy to see why fairy tales would be an attractive genre for a writer whose own use of literary references aims for much the same effect.

Fairy tale motifs appear in a number of Carter's novels, including *The Magic Toyshop*, *Nights at the Circus*, and *Wise Children*. As a way of demonstrating her postmodern approach, though, it is helpful to have a specific example. "Ashputtle or The Mother's Ghost" provides, as the subtitle says, "three versions of one story,"[10] although there is not, in fact, a single version of "Ashputtle," but a variety of tellings called "Aschenpottle," "Ashiepattle," "Cinderella," and many other names. Although she refers to one story, Carter's three versions here add to the store of already-told tales and so draw the reader's attention to the impossibility of fixing on a single origin.

The first of Carter's trilogy is called "The Mutilated Girls," and it is the one whose postmodern elements are most clear. This is a multilayered text, telling the tale of Ashputtle while pondering the other ways in which it might be told, and providing a practical, ironic, and critical commentary upon the events. The text's own genre, therefore, is complex: it is part story, part speculation, and part theory. The story begins with the word "But" ("A," 390), as though the narrator has been in conversation—as, indeed, she would have to have been in order to tell this story—with the narrative voices of the other versions. Beginning in this way draws the reader's attention to the existence of the other stories and thus, in a word, acknowledges both the historical context and this version's difference from it. In the opening sentence, the narrator muses about the story's critical reception, that it could center either on the mutilated sisters, "a story about cutting bits off women, so that they will *fit in*," or on the mother, who is nonetheless "just about to exit the narrative because she is at death's door" ("A," 390). The sentence ends with a quotation, presumably referring to one of the previous versions of "Ashputtle," and this device adds to the contexts within which "Ashputtle" is told, while simultaneously distancing the present version from them. One version of a fairy tale may figuratively quote from others, but to make the quotation literal means that the story we are reading both is and is not itself a story: quotation is more often the province of critical works. Last, the opening sentence makes it very clear that telling, reading, or listening to tales are processes that require active engagement. Both writer and receiver participate in historical contexts that will determine how the participants write and read, and the fairy tale is a very clear example of this. Readers reading Carter's "Ashputtle" will recognize, within the first few lines, that this is a familiar story whose conventions determine a particular way of reading it. To some extent, however, this would also happen in the reception of most literary works because readers have certain expectations about genres or authors that come from personal, literary, and social history. This version, however, undermines any expectations the reader might have of what a fairy tale might be. The narrator makes it clear that there are several ways to read, and to write, "Ashputtle." To question the inevitability of the story's conventions, and to look at what these might tacitly be revealing about (as in this case) the position of woman, is to change the very nature of the story.

Within the first sentence, "Ashputtle" has raised issues important to postmodernism, such as historical context, generic expectations, and the

relationship between reader, author, and story. "Ashputtle" draws attention to itself as fiction, while at the same time pointing out that fiction
can also contain critical commentary. The narrator interprets the story
from a particular, feminist, perspective, although the pedagogical tone
of the narrative voice certainly indicates that Carter's text is also an
instruction in detailed reading. For example, the narrator queries the
father's presence in the story: "Is he so besotted with his new wife that
he cannot see how his daughter is soiled with kitchen refuse?" ("A,"
391). Asking such a question reveals the story's hidden assumptions and
also addresses the reader's critical acumen. Some speculations, however,
are inappropriate because they would change the character of the story
rather than revealing what is contained within it. The narrator, for
example, considers whether the stepdaughters might be the father's
"natural" daughters, but to answer this question, she observes, would
transform "Ashputtle" "from the bare necessity of fairy tale . . . to the
emotional and technical complexity of bourgeois realism" ("A," 392).
Nonetheless, there is a certain irony to this statement because the "bare
necessity" of the fairy tale *is* changed by this rendition. Making the
tale's assumptions explicit changes the possibility of future readings,
including readings of Carter's versions of "Ashputtle" that follow this
one. By placing this critical commentary first, our readings of the more
conventional tales that follow will certainly be more informed, and our
own assumptions about reading fairy tales and indeed about reading any
tales may well be altered. Writing from within the genre, Carter has
read the genre against itself. She makes its assumptions explicit,
includes the reader as a conspirator, and teaches the reader how to read
actively and critically. This didactic element is very much a part of postmodern practice. Whereas its aim is not to replace the assumptions it
questions, the very act of questioning has a subversive potential that
both Carter and postmodernism wish to exploit.

Time, History, and Narrative

Carter does not begin her fairy tales with "once upon a time," the phrase
that clearly signals the reader's entry into a fictional world set in an
unspecified long ago. The open endings of many of her novels indicate a
fluid boundary between the world of fiction and the world of the reader
that fits very clearly into Carter's didactic purpose. The particular time
of any of her novels may not always be specified, but each work is given
a historical context by her many references to other works of fiction.

Time is important in her fiction both in the images she uses to represent time and in the temporal structures of her narratives. Because her writing is so concerned with history, it is hardly surprising that time should play a large role in it, although that role is as multidimensional as one would expect from a vision as complex as Carter's.

Time is something we measure by both natural and mechanical means. The movement of the sun, the cycle of seasons, and the stars, as well as clocks, watches, and computers, are all used to structure an ineffable concept. In order to measure time, in fact, we must use spatial metaphors such as the movement of the hands of a clock around the dial, or the position of the stars in the sky. Different cultures have different ways of perceiving time, as Carter shows in *Nights at the Circus;* therefore even objective, mechanical devices such as clocks tell time in a way that has been culturally determined. A clock imposes an arbitrary order on time, and that we note time's passing with ever more precise clocks expresses something significant about our culture. In *The Passion of New Eve,* Mother describes time as phallic, and in *Nights at the Circus*, Fevvers and Lizzie name their clock Father Time. Their notion of time is derived from Western perceptions and metaphors, which equate time with power. Because time is so hard to describe in any subjective sense, objective methods—seconds, minutes, and hours—are used to symbolize how time functions. This way of dividing time into units has a history associated with economics and with work. Words such as efficiency, productivity, progress, and discipline are all connected to the way in which we divide time and the way in which we measure ourselves against it. In *The Magic Toyshop*, Melanie raises this connection when her tyrannical uncle's watch chain reminds her of something an uncaring Victorian pit owner might have worn. One of the reasons why the Doctor in *The Infernal Desire Machines of Doctor Hoffman* wishes to change his world's relationship to time and history is that to regulate time is to control the very social order by which we live. Were one able to do what the Doctor prescribes, the whole social fabric would be altered; as the Doctor's pictures of Trotsky composing the *Eroica* Symphony and Van Gogh writing *Wuthering Heights* demonstrate, to change our perception of time is to change our view of history.

Using mechanical, rather than natural, indicators to measure time's passing focuses the mind on an inexorable forward movement rather than on a cycle of return and repetition and is therefore tied to ideas of progress. Realist fiction often mirrors this in its largely linear structure, in which the reader and character move forward through an accumula-

tion of detail to knowledge. In Carter's novels, however, neither time
nor progress is so straightforward. One of Carter's most typical narrative
modes is drawn from the conventions of the picaresque. In this genre, a
character's journey through time and space is traditionally connected to
his or her psychological journey. Over time, and as a result of adventures, the character learns to think and behave differently, to develop,
and to progress from ignorance to enlightenment. *The Passion of New Eve*
and *The Infernal Desire Machines of Doctor Hoffman* certainly use the conventions of the picaresque, but whether the characters in these novels
learn or progress is difficult to determine because Carter seems more
interested in raising questions about the very nature of knowledge and
progress. Her novels draw attention to this questioning because their
temporal movement is so complex. The narrative method of these two
novels is retrospective, and therefore, in the most simple sense, a forward movement is complicated by the narrators' looking back on their
lives. In both novels, even the narrative voice itself is difficult to pin
down. Eve is a woman who has been a man. The narration of her life as
a man is complicated by the indeterminate time between her having
been a man and her recounting her experiences as a woman. Although
she has changed, whether her change is a development of her character,
a movement forward, is a decision for the individual reader.

A similar problem attends Desiderio in *The Infernal Desire Machines of
Doctor Hoffman* because in almost every episode he disguises his identity.
He tells the story as a man for whom the past holds the memories of the
love and loss of Albertina, and the future holds only death. In neither
novel is knowledge gained simply through a linear, temporal progression; time, by itself, has not been a teacher. In the course of both novels,
even though the reader is reading sequentially, the narrative moves forward and backward.

The reader's and the narrator's times are conflated in *The Passion of
New Eve* when Eve, looking back on herself as a man, tells the story of
his approaching Beulah, the underground city where the transformation
from he to she takes place. For the reader, the transformation is in the
future, a few pages on; for the narrator, the event has already happened:
"It will become the place where I was born."[11] This sentence is a particularly helpful example of Carter's involving the reader in her fiction.
Because, for the narrator, the operation *has* already happened, for whom
will it happen? Clearly Eve's previously male body is not yet female in
this scene, although the narrator's body is female. Through the reader,
the two bodies come together because the reader will read the transfor-

mation of one into the other. The sentence combines future and past tenses that are made present by the act of reading.

Nights at the Circus also complicates the picaresque genre. When Walser first encounters Fevvers and Lizzie, they trick him into thinking that time is not moving at all. Father Time is always frozen with its hands on 12, and during Walser's interview with Fevvers, even Big Ben seems to strike midnight three times in the course of the night. When the circus train is derailed in the Siberian wilderness, Lizzie and Fevvers lose Father Time and have no mechanical means of measuring time. Consequently, characters' subjective experiences determine their perceptions of the passing of time. Fevvers and Lizzie, for example, see Walser from a distance; although they have calculated that only a week has gone by since the accident, Walser's full beard would indicate that for him time has passed more slowly. In each of these novels, time is in a state of flux, which is only added to by Carter's references to other literature; the characters move backward and forward through time, and against a background of literary history. Despite the field Carter creates in which past and present merge, she is not interested in timelessness, but in giving the present a context drawn from a number of histories. Like Doctor Hoffman, she is interested in changing readers' perceptions of time and history, but unlike him, she does not dictate the specific ways in which this change will happen.

In not one of Carter's novels is there a consistently functioning clock. In *Several Perceptions,* Joseph tries to kill himself using gas but unfortunately lights a match and creates an explosion. As a result, his clock stops, and this, along with his depression, makes him feel as though time itself is frozen. At the end of the novel, he makes his peace with time after a magical party where he discovers that the past need not be a debilitating influence on the present. In this novel, as well as in *Shadow Dance*, the past is a landscape filled with decay. In both novels, time's passing becomes a refrain that appears to draw attention to the passage of time while actually indicating stasis within the narrative. In *Shadow Dance,* the past is represented by the junk shop and the ravaged buildings whose odds and ends are pillaged for sale. Characters in this novel who see the past only as garbage have a similarly skewed view of the present, and some of the novel's cruelty can perhaps be explained by this attitude. Carter's own use of the past in terms of its literary icons is contrasted in this novel with Honeybuzzard's treatment of the past. History has nothing to say to Honeybuzzard; he is interested in it only for reasons of parody or economy. Despite being surrounded by monuments of

the past, he lives entirely in the present, and his disconnection from the
past allows him to live easily with his cruelty.

In *Love*, Annabel is terrified by the juxtaposition of the sun and the
moon in the sky. The temporal distortion this juxtaposition would seem
to indicate is mirrored in the narrative itself, which is not at all sequential. When Annabel makes her first suicide attempt, it is hard to determine a time line of the events leading up to or following the attempt.
The narrator makes the point that in time, all the actors in this drama
came together to create a sequence, although this event does not actually appear in the story. When Annabel throws her husband's alarm
clock into the garbage, it is an indication of her descent into an inner
world where time has become irrelevant. By including an afterword in
which the characters' lives are updated, Carter is pointing to time passing and encouraging the reader to read the present lives she creates in
terms of the past ones. Annabel's solipsism makes time unnecessary to
her, just as Joseph's depression freezes time for him.

Heroes and Villains is the first of Carter's speculative fictions in which
time is an entirely narrative issue without an external referent. The
novel takes place in an unspecified future, although as a dystopia, this
future is designed to have relevance to the reader's present. For Marianne, time is frozen because the world as the reader knows it has ceased
to exist. Mechanical time, as is shown by Marianne's father's clock, has
no reference to anything, and Marianne thinks of the clock as a kind of
pet, because she cannot envision any other function for it. Because the
enclave in which she lives is largely agrarian, the seasons have more
direct bearing on the determination of time. Her father and the other
professors are intellectuals whose research is based on a time before the
apocalypse. They are rooted in the past but cannot make any connection
between past and future. When Marianne's father is killed, she drowns
his clock, and with it her association to his world.

In *Wise Children*, time is, in a sense, compressed: the action takes
place over a single day. During this day, however, Dora Chance revisits
over 100 years of family history, at the same time making numerous
allusions to a literary history extending from the time of Shakespeare.
Birthdays are the time markers Dora uses to anchor her narrative, and it
is significant that the story is set on April 23, the birthday Dora, her
twin sister Nora, their father, and their uncle share with Shakespeare.
Their grandfather clock, which has always been off by one hour, chooses
the date of Dora and Nora's 75th birthday to chime the hours correctly.
Age, here, makes Dora particularly conscious of time, and though she

makes several references to her proximity to death, even mortality is cheated by the end of the novel. Time in *Wise Children* takes detours rather than moving in the linear fashion that might be implied by birthdays. Each birthday is, in fact, a reminder of the past, and of the complications of the twins' genesis. Each is a marker of change, but also of repetition and return. Birthdays provide opportunities to comment on the history of the twentieth century, which, because it is narrated from Dora's perspective, also intertwines public and personal histories. The various events she mentions seem to happen not so much as linear cause and effect as in a series of archeological narrative layers where all times seem to happen at once; Dora cheerfully admits that she cannot keep the story straight. Despite Dora's being specific about birthdays, the ages of her associates and her family, and the public events through which they live, there is a sense of the fairy tale in her narrative, and "once upon a time" is a phrase she uses to introduce her memories of the dancing classes that began her career on the stage. Here "Once upon a time" signals that what is to follow is fiction; Dora makes it clear that she misremembers some things, and that other memories are overlaid with dreams and hopes that may have had nothing to do with the actual moment. The absurd and the ordinary intertwine in such a way that time itself seems to become magical. One of the ways this is evidenced is in the ages of the characters, who, although they add on years, do not seem to age in the usual sense. Thus Dora's uncle's being a magician cannot in itself account for his extraordinary health and virility; on his 100th birthday, he is still as hearty and as sexually active as he was when he was much younger. Dora's explanation for this is that love alters sight, and because she is telling the story and loves her uncle, she registers no significant change over time. For her, he is as he was as a young man because that is when she first loved him.

Time in *Wise Children* is figured within the context of performance and is thus a very different kind of time than that determined by clocks. Just as Fevvers's aerial somersaults seem to cheat time and gravity by being performed much more slowly than would literally be possible, so Dora's narrative is connected to the artificial time of the stage. Each birthday, for example, is marked by some connection with performing arts. On their 7th, the twins are taken to their first movie; on their 13th, their uncle takes them to their father's dressing room in the theater where he is playing Macbeth. On their 17th, the twins' father invites them to perform in his musical tribute to Shakespeare. An unspecified birthday, signaled only by the present Nora receives from her beloved Tony, happens during the filming of *A Midsummer Night's Dream*, and the final, 75th birthday takes place on camera at their father's party for his 100th. That each of these birthdays is also marked by sexual performance is, perhaps, Dora's bawdy pun. Performance in the theater and particularly, as Dora says, on celluloid can cheat time's forward motion as, one might argue, can fiction. Because Dora's narrative is structured in five acts like a Shakespearean play, her narrative too can change the perception of time as a forward trajectory. As Carter does with regard to pornographic representation, she gives the reader responsibility for changing the nature of time. In the act of reading her novels, past and present exist in an instructive relationship that she must have hoped would lead to an altered future at the novels' ends. Wise children know their history, and equipped with that knowledge, they have some control over what happens next.

Chapter Three

"The Bristol Trilogy":
Shadow Dance, Several Perceptions, and *Love*

In her essay "Truly, It Felt Like Year One," Carter muses about the heady intellectual atmosphere of the 1960s, the sexual revolution, the relaxation of manners, and the glamour of "madness, alienation, hating your parents."[1] In the midst of "a great deal of unrestrained and irreverent frivolity," however, Carter writes that "towards the end of the sixties it started to feel like living on a demolition site—one felt one was living on the edge of the unimaginable: there was a constant sense of fear and excitement and, of course, it was to do with war" ("Year One," 211–12). It is this latter atmosphere that Carter chooses to explore in *Shadow Dance* (1966), *Several Perceptions* (1968), and *Love* (1971), her first, third, and fifth novels. All three are studies in dissipation, death, and cruelty, and although these novels do not occupy the same magical terrain as Carter's more speculative fictions, they do consider the oppressive and liberating aspects of language as well as its transformative power. There is a continuity of interest in Carter's work, even though she adopts different styles in other novels. Her interest in various aspects of performance, her feminism, and her irreverence are all evident in the Bristol Trilogy.[2]

Shadow Dance

Plot and Characters

Although it is an undeniable cliché to point to an author's first novel as containing the nascent glimmerings of later brilliance, *Shadow Dance* does indeed explore themes, images, and ideas with which readers of Carter's later work will be familiar. In writing about *Shadow Dance*, Anthony Burgess praised Carter for "looking at the mess of contemporary life without flinching,"[3] and this is a comment as appropriate to her first novel as to her last. The mess might not have changed much, but Carter looked at it with an ever more prismatic eye.

This first novel has been largely ignored by literary critics.[4] Its style veers closer to realism than is the case in her later works, where realism is most often the subject of parody. For readers whose familiarity with Carter is based on her fantastic tales of winged aerialists or desire machines, this novel will seem more prosaic. Despite the bleakness of the novel's plot, however, the magic resides in what one reviewer called "a dark luxuriance of bizarre images,"[5] and another described as "energetic, overdecorated prose that she maintains at a very even, cool temperature."[6] *Shadow Dance* is evidence of Carter's characteristic concern with the material world as she explains it in "Notes from the Front Line": "*this* world is all that there is, and in order to question the nature of reality one must move from a strongly grounded base in what constitutes material reality. . . . I believe that all myths are products of the human mind and reflect only aspects of material human practice."[7]

Shadow Dance is a novel as cluttered with the imagery of junk and rubbish as is the seedy antique shop that serves as the novel's main setting. The proprietors, Morris Gray and Honeybuzzard, spend their time scrounging in derelict houses for salable remnants. Morris is a failed painter who escapes from his dreary life with his wife Edna into pretense or fantasy or junk-induced euphoria: "he loved to nose questingly among the abandoned detritus of other people's lives for oddments, fragments, bits of this and that."[8] He has carious teeth, a face like "an El Greco Christ" (*SD*, 9), and useless but elaborate sympathies for the hardships of strangers and acquaintances.

In contrast to gray Morris, Honeybuzzard glitters with sexual ambiguity and theatricality. He is a great performer, who slips in and out of various roles, from childlike innocent to sexual sadist. Playful and beautiful, he has "the soft, squashy-nosed, full-lipped face one associates with angels blowing glad, delirious trumpets in early Florentine pictures of the Nativity" (*SD*, 57). But his childish delight in joke-shop items, plastic snot, false noses, vampire teeth, and exploding cigarettes (*SD*, 76–77) barely conceals an equal pleasure in impersonal cruelty. Manipulation and power are his favorite games, and he plays them with a combination, as his name would suggest, of charm and voraciousness. He makes paper jumping jacks resembling his friends (*SD*, 81, 127), wishes to "play chess with men and women" as pieces (*SD*, 119), and imagines "an exploding contraceptive" (*SD*, 77) to add to his store of jokes. Morris, from whose point of view the novel is narrated, comments that for

Honeybuzzard "even sex was a joke, a savage one" (*SD*, 77). And Honeybuzzard treats as a joke even the most vile of his actions, knifing and brutally disfiguring the face of his former lover, Ghislaine, who, in a frenzy of self-abasement, continues to pursue him. Released from the hospital, she hovers on the fringes of people's sympathy and in Morris's nightmares. Only Honeybuzzard seems nonchalant about what he has done, although he is perversely amused by her letters of forgiveness, seeing in them an opportunity for further mischief.

Ghislaine's conversation with Morris begins the novel, but she is largely absent from the rest of it. The circumstances of her disfigurement remain a mystery, although Morris, who is certain that Honeybuzzard was the perpetrator, nonetheless finds Ghislaine far more frightening. Morris is so terrified of contact with her that he flees from even her imagined presence and, in doing so, admits his complicity in her attack. Blaming her for the failure of their one sexual liaison, he once handed her over to Honeybuzzard, saying "'Take her and teach her a lesson'" (*SD*, 34, 37). The consequences of his "sort of joke" (*SD*, 37) multiply horribly, leading to suicide, despair, and eventually Ghislaine's ritualized murder at Honeybuzzard's hands.

Imagery and Narrative Method

The novel's material and symbolic interest in collecting bits of this and that mirrors Carter's narrative style, one that continues throughout her corpus. Carter uses a technique called "intertextuality," a term coined by Julia Kristeva to describe the way in which one text will make shorthand references to others, thus allowing for multiple levels of reading and meaning: "any text is constructed as a mosaic of quotations; any text is the absorption and transformation of another."[9] "Life imitates art" (*SD*, 61), as Honeybuzzard is fond of saying, but then, so does art imitate and draw on other art. For example, the staff in the café that Morris frequents are called "Struldbrugs," a reference to the pitiable characters in the third book of Jonathan Swift's *Gulliver's Travels* (1726).[10] Though immortal, the Struldbrugs are not blessed with eternal youth, and because they age horribly, they are objects of scorn and revulsion. Carter's equally withered Struldbrugs contribute to the novel's atmosphere of decay. They are all women who have lost their youth and beauty and have no value without them: from Morris's point of view, for example, they are "creatures" (*SD*, 30), only barely recognizable as women. Like Ghislaine, they are dehumanized by their appearance.

Swift's protagonist, Gulliver, is the reader's emissary in a world of fantastic creations, and so readers may have sympathy with his points of view, although these become more and more untenable as the novel progresses. Like Gulliver, Morris may evoke our sympathy, particularly when compared to the perverse Honeybuzzard. Nevertheless, he shows his own cruelty in his treatment of Edna and his cowardice when faced with Ghislaine. These levels of meaning may not be necessary to a perfectly adequate understanding of the novel; however, the "snag," as Carter put it, is that she does "put everything in a novel to be read—read the way allegory was intended to be read . . . on as many levels as you can comfortably cope with at the time."[11] Carter's novels consistently make reference to literary genres and works as well as to texts that have made significant cultural or historical contributions, writings by Freud, Marx, and Sade, for example. Carter is most often irreverent in her treatment of these texts, and they become part of the cultural and literary symbolism that she continually subjects to close scrutiny.

Carter's language is luxuriant with bizarre images, and she draws attention to language through combinations that acknowledge her debt to the surrealists. Like them, she wished to create "juxtapositions of objects, or people, or ideas, that arbitrarily extend our notions of the connections it is possible to make."[12] The junk shop, Honeybuzzard's room above it, and the derelict house provide material evidence of these connections. Each of these settings contains images of the past; Honeybuzzard and Morris are especially keen on Victoriana to use as bait for tourists. But in each case, what might once have been solemn, serious, or sacred is parodied or profaned. Both Honeybuzzard and Carter are iconoclastic, but whereas Carter's concern is to question the underlying reasons as to why certain images become cherished and inviolable, Honeybuzzard's interest is literal and superficial, and his desire is to shock. Thus, he litters items in the junk shop with false red noses. He collects parodies of the Nativity, patriotism, and Queen Victoria, as well as advertisements for corsets and bustles, to pin on his wall. Among his possessions are a skull from a plague pit (*SD*, 100) and a "jar containing a pickled foetus" (*SD*, 101). His room is a surrealist collage, and like the surrealists, Honeybuzzard lives "on the edge of the senses; of perpetual outrage and scandal" ("Alchemy," 69) although he lacks surrealism's "faith in humankind's ability to recreate itself; the conviction that struggle *can* bring something better" ("Alchemy," 67). There is, nonetheless, violence in surrealism's yoking together of disparate images, and this violence attracts Honeybuzzard.

Honeybuzzard seeks dead matter in order to consume it, not to re-create it. He is hungry for control, so he destroys images that imply power or incite reverence. In the derelict house where Honeybuzzard murders Ghislaine, he and Morris discover religious objects: rosaries, prayer books, and a plaster Christ. All of this makes Honeybuzzard think of Ghislaine, whose father, he tells Morris, is a clergyman. Ghislaine has been associated several times with religious imagery. Drinking a beer she has bought for him, Morris suddenly feels he is "drinking her down sacramentally" (*SD*, 5). Later, he describes her as looking "like a holy image" (*SD*, 7). Even Ghislaine's name associates her with the sacred; it is a feminization of the name of a seventh-century saint, although Ghislaine herself would hardly qualify for the title.[13] The sacred images in the house, however, rouse Honeybuzzard to increasing violence, and he imagines chaining Ghislaine "to that symbol of her father over there and raping her" (*SD*, 134–35).

Honeybuzzard's vandalism of the past directly contrasts Carter's use of it. Whereas the author's aim is always to question, "to find out what certain configurations of imagery in our society, in our culture, really stand for,"[14] the character's aim is to acknowledge the power of those images through wholesale destruction of them. By associating Honey-buzzard with the surrealists, for whom she had some admiration, Carter is pointing to the difference between questioning and destroying, and to the power, the very materiality, of language.

Women and Other Garbage

As liberating as language can be, however, its materiality can also oppress. The religious imagery in the novel paints men as angels or Christ figures, but women as suffering saints or objects to be consumed. It is not surprising that women are so often associated with food: Emily is fruitcake, Ghislaine is sacramental wine, Edna and Emily cook, the Struldbrug serves food in the café. Sexuality becomes a parody of com-munion, as the vampire motif associated with both Honeybuzzard and Ghislaine implies. Honeybuzzard finds religious images powerful; they incite his increasing perversity because they seem to sanction his treat-ment of women.

In "Notes from the Front Line," Carter writes that in the late 1960s, she came to an awareness "of the nature of [her] reality as a *woman*"; throughout her writing, therefore, she explores the imagery that creates the "social fictions" of women's lives ("Notes," 70). *Shadow Dance* seems to explore the social images that, most disturbingly, make women complicit in their own victimization. In later novels, Carter will portray women as strong enough to rise above oppression, but here she is documenting the various forms that oppression can take. Ghislaine's suffering culminates in her confession to Honeybuzzard: "I've learned my lesson, I can't live without you, you are my master, do what you like with me" (SD, 169). Edna's more domestic masochism is described as Victorian, when "girls were gentle and meek . . . and laid their tender napes beneath a husband's booted foot" (SD, 45). Only Emily resists the pattern, despite finding herself pregnant with Honeybuzzard's child. Emily is strong, practical, and self-possessed, although the novel suggests that these qualities result from androgyny: "one might almost have taken her for a boy dressed up as a girl" (SD, 67). Conversely, Honeybuzzard's increasing madness corresponds to his increased and stereotypical feminization. From peevish temper tantrums to carrying lipstick, he is compared to mad Ophelia after he murders Ghislaine, and he cradles the plaster Christ in his arms as if it were a baby.

Truly affectionate and inviolable relationships seem only to happen between men. Women exist for sex, but not for friendship. When Honeybuzzard describes Morris as "David to my Jonathan" (SD, 58), he seems to be assuming a true bond of affection, although Honeybuzzard's psychopathic behavior is a perplexing basis for such closeness. Nonetheless, one aspect of the biblical story that does seem appropriate comes from David's lament over the death of Jonathan: "I am distressed for thee, my brother Jonathan: very pleasant hast thou been unto me: thy love to me was wonderful, passing the love of women" (2 Samuel 1:26). The friendship between Morris and Honeybuzzard seems to take this model literally, using it as a foundation for excluding women from any true friendship.

Women can, in fact, be detrimental to the fraternity. Morris and Honeybuzzard's dance in one of the derelict houses ends, not because of Honeybuzzard's "fierce embrace" (SD, 95), but because Morris, who has been lulled into a dreamlike state, imagines that it is Ghislaine who clings to him. In terror at this vision, he flings Honeybuzzard away, and they flee the house because they feel it has asserted an evil will. It is Emily who calls the police, despite Morris's attempts to stop her, after she and Morris discover Ghislaine's body. Although Morris has abandoned his wife with ease and relief, he feels he cannot betray his friend, so he returns to the house and to Honeybuzzard.

Morris and Honeybuzzard have a more than economic interest in rubbish; indeed, they revel in the leavings of other people's lives. Moreover, there is a sinister implication to their hobby, because it generalizes to include their treatment of women, who are equally objects to be used and discarded. Morris "gives" Ghislaine to Honeybuzzard, attempts to steer Edna into bed with Oscar, and is eventually relieved that his neglect has allowed Henry Glass to "inherit" (*SD,* 160) her. The painting he creates of "a decaying female form, dead, in a brown desert" (*SD,* 124) makes the connection explicit, echoing Morris's association of Ghislaine with a Francis Bacon painting "of flesh as a disgusting symbol of the human condition" (*SD,* 20). The houses Morris and Honeybuzzard pillage are symbolic equivalents to the women in their lives because both are treated as carrion. Once the excitement of the new find has been exhausted, the houses, like the women, are abandoned to demolition.

Shadow Dance is a bleak novel. The only moment of relief comes when Morris discovers that the Struldbrug he fears has been killed by Honeybuzzard's childish actions has been resurrected. Carter's writing is a brilliant, funny evocation of joy, and it foreshadows the sort of writing for which she is justly admired: "Deep notes of joy rang from the cream horns. The eclairs—eclairissement—burst under the pressure of the sweet white cream of joy. The ham rolls bounded like ecstatic piglets from their Cellophane pens" (*SD,* 163). Her later novels do not, of course, abandon their critique of "social fictions" ("Notes," 70), but their language draws readers' attention to wonder as well as despair. In "The Alchemy of the Word," Carter explains that she gave up on the surrealists because "they were not good with women" ("Alchemy," 73). But "the old juices can still run . . . when I hear that most important of all surrealist principles: 'The marvellous alone is beautiful' " ("Alchemy," 73). Carter's deep intellectual engagement with issues such as violence and sexism continues to be paramount in her fiction and nonfiction, but her interest in the marvelous seems to imply that the world she wishes to change is worth the effort.

Several Perceptions

Like *Shadow Dance, Several Perceptions* is set in a decaying landscape. The third-person narrative is filtered through Joseph Harker, a hospital orderly who suffers from debilitating dreams and decides, in the first chapter, to kill himself. His attempt fails because he lights a match in a room filled with gas, and the resulting explosion blows out the windows. He is obsessed with the Vietnam War, about which he dreams, reads books, and collects newspaper clippings. His immediate acquaintances are a ragtag group of the downtrodden. Old Sunny plays an imaginary violin. Viv has no work and lives with his mother, Mrs. Boulder, whose profits from being "on the game" disappear in the bottle. Cheerful Beverley Kyte, called Kay, looks after his dying mother in a "great Georgian palace friable with worm and rot."[15] Anne Blossom lives downstairs from Joseph and summons the ambulance after the explosion. She has a painful limp, a sour manner, and is in mourning for her baby, whom she has recently given up for adoption.

This is not a novel of plot. Nothing much happens, and what does happen is not explained in any conventional narrative sequence. The characters pass randomly through each other's lives and come together at a Christmas Eve party in an extraordinarily optimistic denouement. For Marc O'Day, the novel explores the "disorientation and discontinuity of the mid-1960s countercultural mind and lifestyle. Joseph the dreamer and his friends and acquaintances are a whimsically individualised provincial counterculture in its high period of waywardness, excess and flowering."[16] As O'Day also points out, this specificity of interest caused one of the novel's reviewers to suggest that *Several Perceptions* was too "fashionable" and "circumstantial."[17] The novel, though, is more than a period piece. It is also more than what Richard Boston calls "a powerful account of the horror, the logic and the poetry of a schizophrenic's world,"[18] although the novel may indeed celebrate the discontinuity of a schizophrenic world.

The Carnival of Style

Despite the misery surrounding Joseph, *Several Perceptions* is a remarkably cheerful book. In fact, its wry humor stands out against a background of newspaper reports of mutilated children and characters whose lives have been decimated by war or who are dying painful deaths. O'Day writes that the novel "demonstrates a precise and even touching hold on conventional codes for representing reality,"[19] but the novel's logic is rather more dreamlike than realist. It gives the illusion of a random structure that, one might argue, is closer to being "lifelike" than to traditional codes of realism, but it is, most of all, a novel that emphasizes its literariness especially through its verbal pyrotechnics. Carter's baroque language creates layers of meaning, images upon images, so that everything in the novel seems to be in flux. This fluid style seems to mitigate against the initial absolutism of Joseph's despair. The novel's optimism does not deny the seriousness of his condition, nor does such optimism suggest a frivolous attitude toward the effects of poverty or of war, both of which have had destructive consequences to characters in the novel. Carter's dark comedy always involves a lack of liberal-humanist reverence. She combines the hushed tones of a graveside manner with the gleeful celebration of a wake. Joseph's suicide attempt, for example, is tragicomic: "He struck a match. 'Gas is funny stuff,' said the lugubrious fellow who mended the fire, 'you never know where you are with gas.' " (*SP*, 21). This quick and humorous transition suggests that readers not linger over Joseph's narcissistic angst. Carter often insists that readers are able to hold two or more, sometimes contradictory, beliefs simultaneously. Joseph's actions are both serious and ridiculous, despairing and funny, social protest and solipsism.

Carter's language suggests the image of a palimpsest in that the language creates layers upon layers of meaning. For example, the description of Old Sunny that begins the novel is of a man who has seen better days. His clothes are shabby: "grave-clothes small-clothes flapped around his legs like small, brown dogs." His eyes are peevishly red, "as if he were angry at being so old"; his fingers are "knotted"; and his skin is like a "purplish stretch of plucked fowl" (*SP*, 1–2). Yet this sad portrait is overlaid with another. Sunny is entranced by the imagined music, and his fingers "quivered like the wings of a humming bird": "All was gilded with visionary sunset light and the little old man appeared irradiated and just dropped from heaven. He was playing an imaginary fiddle as Joseph had seen him do before. Raptly he serenaded the tree, which dropped leaves on his head from time to time as if tossing contemptuous pennies. Beneath his feet, moist autumn grass blandly gleamed" (*SP*, 1). This plethora of images gives Sunny a series of identities. Although dressed like a tramp, he is also a strange angel to whom the trees and the grass respond, and through his performance, he is transformed. Indeed Joseph, who is "glimpsing immense cracks in the structure of the real world" (*SP*, 2), feels that he might almost begin to see the fiddle and hear the music.

Throughout the novel, Carter's language also seems to create cracks in the structure of the real world. In this way, she communicates Joseph's state of mind but also indicates that there are always several perceptions of any situation. Whether Joseph is technically schizophrenic, he is certainly on the fringes of madness. He feels threatened by the claws of crabs in the fishmonger's, menaced by his parents' house, and tortured by dreams in which the murderers and maniacs turn out to be himself. His room is as dirty and unkempt as is Joseph himself, and after his suicide attempt, he is so truculent and self-absorbed that he wallows in filth. The explosion has stopped his alarm clock, and time itself seems to Joseph to be confused; moreover, not having died, Joseph feels that he has "stumbled upon a formula that annihilated causation and now anything was possible, rain would fall upwards and sparrows begin to recite the Apocalypse" (*SP*, 22). Cause and effect, one of the staples of realism, is given short shrift in this novel. From Joseph's perspective, perhaps, this might be because the violence, particularly that of the Vietnam War, he sees in the world around him has destroyed any logic to events. The world seems like a bad dream because nightmare and waking life have merged. But the novel's optimism would seem to indicate that this is only one possibility. Just as the language suggests multiple perspectives, so a structure based on chance and discontinuities transgresses any singular viewpoint. Here, reality is neither fixed nor certain, and this uncertainty leads to a carnival atmosphere in which anything seems possible.

Performance

Performative play, rather than being frivolous, recognizes that identity is subject to cultural myths. In a number of Carter's novels, transgression against authority is associated with images of performance, and the theater and the circus are the two sources of such imagery in *Several Perceptions*. "Self" is a kind of spectacle, and rather than being fixed, Carter's characters take on different roles. In *Shadow Dance*, Honeybuzzard introduces this theme to Carter's work: "I like—you know—to slip in and out of me. I would like to be somebody different each morning. Me and not-me. I would like to have a cupboard bulging with all different bodies and faces and choose a fresh one every morning" (*SD*, 79). For the sinister Honeybuzzard, this is a way of escaping responsibility for his gruesome actions; in later novels, characters who are "me and not-me" are responding to the social fictions to which Carter refers in "Notes from the Front Line."

The epigraph to the novel, taken from David Hume, raises the connection between the novel's performative imagery and its discontinuous structure: "The mind is a kind of theatre, where several perceptions successively make their appearance, pass, re-pass, glide away and mingle in an infinite variety of postures and situations." Ransome, Joseph's psychiatrist, calls Joseph "a bad actor" (*SP*, 67). Rather than translating his anger at the Vietnam War into any kind of real action, Joseph creates a complex role for himself as both victim and perpetrator of violence. He begins by giving away his clothes and money, so that he begins to look and act like a tramp. Carter uses various allusions, in fact, to align Joseph with literary victims. His name associates him with Joseph the dreamer, who is sold by his brothers to the Ishmaelites (Genesis 37:28). His last name, Harker, connects him to Jonathan Harker in Bram Stoker's *Dracula*, who is imprisoned in Dracula's castle and made the plaything of three vampire women. It is not surprising that Joseph describes his former love, Charlotte, as having "lips of treacherous vampire redness and a wet mouth which was a mantrap of ivory fangs" (*SP*, 16). Among Joseph's books is a copy of Lewis Carroll's *Alice in Wonderland*. Like Alice, Joseph journeys through a disorienting landscape that is alternately confusing and threatening. But Joseph is hardly an innocent. He has burned books in libraries and chalked "SUPPORT YOUR NEIGHBOURHOOD ASSASSIN" (*SP*, 4) on a nearby wall. Ransome remarks that Joseph is "beginning to look like an assassin. . . . You look like John Wilkes Booth" (*SP*, 65). For all of his apparent social conscience, Joseph's only action is to present himself as a walking reminder of the hostilities he abhors.

The celebratory aspect of performance is that it suggests a free play of meanings. The performer who is both me and not-me is on a threshold between identities, from which several perceptions may emerge. Joseph collects facts and keeps them pasted in a scrapbook "as if they might help to shore up the crumbling dome of the world" (*SP*, 3), but at the end of the novel, he decides to throw them away. Even facts are contingent on the observer's standpoint; it is the carnivalesque ending, rather than the facts, that allows Joseph to emerge from his depressed state of mind.

A Christmas Truce

The novel ends with a Christmas Eve party at which, as if by a miracle, all wrongs seem to be put right. There is a Christmas truce in the war, and the more domestic hostilities seem also to be assuaged. Reviewing *Several Perceptions*, Richard Boston found the ending troublesome: "after [Carter's] earlier tough-mindedness, one had hoped for a more telling denouement than the Spirit of Christmas."[20] The party takes place in an atmosphere of carnival abandon at the home of Kay's dying mother, a "foot-lights favourite of the 1930s" who had bought "this dilapidated mansion for herself and turned it into a set for the major starring role never offered to her in the actual theatre" (*SP*, 132). As such, the ending seems a fitting culmination to the novel, each of whose characters is in some way associated with performance. Kay, for example, has "the appearance of being in costume" (*SP*, 11), while Viv performs "even the most commonplace acts with the air of a circus acrobat" (*SP*, 25). Joseph describes his dreams as "a three-ring circus" (*SP*, 65) and even sees death as a kind of clown: "[death] was just a practical joker or fool with bells and bladder" (*SP*, 27). Given that the lives and experiences of these characters invoke a kind of spectacle, the Christmas Eve party is entirely in keeping with the themes and images Carter has explored thus far. Just before Joseph goes to the party, he spends an afternoon in bed with Mrs. Boulder, and in her sexual play as well as in her description of her life as a child of fairground people, she introduces the notion of carnival. Like the Christmas truce, carnival is, as Mikhail Bahktin points out, a "temporary liberation from the prevailing truth and from the established order."[21] Bahktin also writes that "moments of death and revival, of change and renewal always [lead] to a festive perception of the world,"[22] and this is the case in *Several Perceptions*, where the celebration of Christ's birth takes place while people await Mrs. Kyte's death. The miraculous events, such as Joseph's making friends with time again or Anne's overcoming her debilitating limp, do not occur in an atmosphere of piety but within a temporary and self-contained celebration of relativity. In keeping with Carter's tragicomic vision, the miracles happen in a rotting and decaying house. However, it would be out of keeping with the rest of the novel were these events to be seen as irrevocable. In a 1992 interview, Carter commented that "the carnival has to stop. The whole point of the feast of fools is that things went on as they did before, after it stopped."[23] Like carnival, the party suggests renewal as part of a process rather than as an end in itself.

In the theatrical world of *Several Perceptions* and in the exhibitionist one of *Shadow Dance*, characters create themselves to be looked at. The costumes worn by both Honeybuzzard and Joseph are specifically intended to make people look at them, so that each character may flaunt his protest against a real or imagined authority. Women's costumes and bodies, however, mark their level of erotic spectacle. Ghislaine's mutilated face draws a different kind of gaze from the one she attracted as a beautiful woman, and yet both of her faces are on view at once: the deformed side of her face is the erasure of the beautiful one. In the end, she appeals to Honeybuzzard to do what he will with her, because in her abject state she has no identity other than the one he has forced upon her. The suffering woman as spectacle is one of the Gothic elements Carter exploits in The Bristol Trilogy. Only Anne Blossom throws off the painful limp she thinks of as a punishment for sex, pregnancy, and abandonment. Ghislaine and Annabel (in *Love*) sink under the weight of a masochism sanctioned by society.

Love

After the rich, descriptive language of *Several Perceptions*, *Love* seems almost clinical. The language is abstract, the settings are stark, and the characters are self-absorbed. Lee, his wife Annabel, and his brother Buzz are an intense, emotionally exclusive triad whose interactions thrive on pain. As Lorna Sage writes, "they construct their selves, cannibalistically, out of each other, and inscribe their meanings on each other's flesh."[24] To love, in this novel, is to consume and to wound, and this thoroughly unlikable trio excel at making savagery into an art form.

Lee is a beautiful, blond, blue-eyed boy who has a wardrobe of smiles he uses to ease his way through life. He wakes up in the aftermath of a New Year's party to find the unknown Annabel in his arms, where she has arbitrarily snuggled for warmth. Because she is friendless and he is sentimental, Lee takes Annabel to live with him, and he falls in love with her because he thinks they share a sense of being strangers in the world. Annabel lives within a private mythology that connects with the external world only at an obtuse angle: "all she apprehended through her senses she took only as objects for interpretation in the expressionist style and she saw, in everyday things, a world of mythic fearful shapes."[25] The opening scene depicts Annabel's terror when she sees the moon and the sun in the sky at the same time. That she has "no instinct for self-preservation if she [is] confronted by ambiguities" (*Love*, 1) suggests that her life will have a tragic end; in Carter's equivocal universe, no one can survive for long without a healthy appreciation for the duplicity of things. Buzz, however, thrives on chaos, especially when he has a hand in creating it. Whereas Annabel can see only iconically and through correspondences to her mythic imaginings, Buzz prefers "the cult of appearances" (*Love*, 25). His camera gives him a voyeur's license, and with it he gains control over everything, including, for a time, his sexual jealousy. Terrified of hidden "fangs or guillotines" (*Love*, 94), he sees Annabel as a *vagina dentata* but desires her as part of his desire to

wound and to penetrate his brother. Buzz and Annabel have an unspoken alliance, although their liaison works only insofar as they are both
connected to Lee, who seeks relief from his mad wife and violent brother
in a series of casual affairs. Their ménage à trois is emotionally hermetic;
no relation between any two characters exists except in response to the
third.

Lee and Buzz have a reputation as "bad boys." They have different
fathers but share a mother who went mad in spectacular fashion, painting her naked body with cabalistic symbols and invading the Empire
Day celebration at Lee's school. The brothers are alienated, exotic, and
self-contained and enjoy self-conscious, public displays of violence and
eroticism. Annabel's intrusion into this symbiotic relation provokes
Buzz to extreme behavior, although Annabel is soon absorbed into
Buzz's imaginings and they become accomplices.

Annabel's suicide, after two attempts, is precipitated by the unsatis-
factory consummation of her fantasies. Despite the pictures of Lee that
cover the wall of Buzz's room, Annabel and Buzz are unable to fulfill
their desire for each other without Lee's presence as both erotic object
and wounded husband. Their failure is a failure of the real to live up to
the imaginary: "When they embraced each other's phantoms, each in
his separate privacy had savoured the most refined of pleasures but, con-
noisseurs of unreality as they were, they could not bear the crude
weight, the rank smell and the ripe taste of real flesh" (Love, 95).

Love and the Gothic

In the afterword to Fireworks, Carter acknowledges her fondness for
Edgar Allan Poe, and her discussion of the Gothic could well be a
description of Love: "The Gothic tradition in which Poe writes grandly
ignores the value systems of our institutions; it deals entirely with the
profane. Its great themes are incest and cannibalism. Character and
event are exaggerated beyond reality, to become symbols, ideas, passions. Its style will tend to be ornate, unnatural—and thus operate
against the perennial human desire to believe the word as fact. Its only
humor is black humor. It retains a singular moral function—that of pro-
voking unease."[26] All of this is true of Love, which, although not a
Gothic novel in the eighteenth-century tradition of Walpole, exemplifies
the estrangement from the ordinary one finds in the tales of Poe or
Hoffman. "We live in Gothic times" (FW, 132), Carter writes, and Love
points out just how Gothic the "days of social mobility and sexual

licence" (*Love*, 113) of the 1960s could be. The Gothic is one response to what Carter sees as the "demolition site" ("Year One," 211) of the end of the 1960s. Rapid social change and "living on the edge of the unimaginable" ("Year One," 211) could certainly produce the sort of disorientation experienced by the characters in *Love*. The "dreadful rebellion of the familiar" (*Love*, 3) can equally herald celebration and madness.

Carter is clearly drawing on Gothic conventions in general as well as making specific references to Poe's work. The novel opens in a ruined park that once surrounded an eighteenth-century mansion. Annabel enjoys the park's "Gothic north" (*Love*, 2), where an ivy-covered tower still remains. Poe's poem "Annabel Lee" (1849) echoes throughout the novel, but it does so ironically, because although the characters' names may be drawn from the poem, the characters' marriage could hardly be described as "as a love that the winged seraphs of heaven / Coveted her and me."[27] Annabel is "otherworldl[y]" (*Love*, 7), as Lee suggests, and although her otherworldliness has more to do with the strangeness of her psychological life than with anything supernatural, madness is certainly a staple of the Gothic tale. Last, the sadomasochism that is common to the Gothic genre is the primary mode of interaction between Annabel, Lee, and Buzz. Although we have no personal history to explain Annabel's madness or desire for self-immolation, her masochism seems a manner by which she creates an identity and secures a partner who will hurt her. In the first part of the novel, she is passive and indifferent. She lies on the floor, staring at the wall for hours on end, although she soon begins to transfer the imagery in her mind to the walls of Lee's white room. After her suicide attempt, she begins to realize that she can use her passivity as a tool both to wound Lee and to gain autonomy: "she knew, if she were clever, she could behave exactly as she wished without censure or reprimand" (*Love*, 75). The added ingredient to their relationship is Lee's guilt. Because the sight of Lee copulating with Carolyn precipitates Annabel's slashing her wrists, she soon learns that her passivity can be used to wield power, and she punishes Lee mercilessly. As Michelle Massé points out, the masochist "achieves a certain amount of active agency through her masochism, in which she controls, accuses or hurts others."[28] Initially, Lee finds Annabel's submission erotic. When he deflowers her, she is limp, though "comforted by memories of the nursery because he undressed her as if she were a little girl" (*Love*, 33). Her subsequent bleeding discomfits Lee, but it gives Annabel a glimpse into the nature of her power: "she soon saw she could hurt him as badly with her silences as he could ever afflict her by any other means" (*Love*, 34). Complicating their sexual congress is that Annabel is wearing Buzz's clothes when Lee decides it is time for her first sexual experience. Incestuous and narcissistic homoeroticism is hardly hidden in the novel, and Buzz aggressively declares his desire for Lee in the afterword. Their physical intimacy, however, most often takes the form of violence. Buzz is prone to hysterical attacks, and Lee can subdue him only by force. Nonetheless, Lee sees Buzz as part of himself; indeed, "he had scarcely differentiated between his brother and himself" (*Love*, 64). In Annabel's passivity, and her desire for "a bland, white motionless face" (*Love*, 4), like that of the woman in the pornographic pictures Buzz gives her, Annabel creates herself as a blank page on which the brothers' desires can be written. Her presence brings these desires to the fore, so that when Buzz seethes in jealous anger while Lee and Annabel have sex, the object of his jealousy may be either or both of them. In this, Annabel echoes Ghislaine from *Shadow Dance*, who also pays the price of disrupting the ambiguous desires of a fraternity.

The initial eroticism of Annabel's submissiveness seems to wear off after the wedding. Lee soon finds another mistress, Carolyn, and in exchanging intimate reflections with her, he relates the story of how he came to beat Annabel. The circumstances of the beating clearly indicate the dynamic between Lee and Annabel. The beating happens over a game of chess. Lee plays with logic, and Annabel with passion, and as Lee comments, "she usually wins" (*Love*, 40). Once, when he has taken her queen, she hits him, so he ties her up and beats her until she is bruised. In recounting the story, Lee is the one in control. He has been inflating the details of the relationship "out of all proportion" (*Love*, 40), and although he regrets doing so, he tells the story in such a way that he appears "in a good light" (*Love*, 41). Annabel's response to the beating is eerie: "She raised a strangely joyous face to him; the pallor of her skin and the almost miraculous lustre of her eyes startled and even awed him. . . . 'That will teach you to take my queen,' she said smugly" (*Love*, 40–41). It is clear that she is the one punishing him. By beating her, Lee has lost control, and through her subordination, Annabel has, paradoxically, won it.

Readers and Voyeurs

In *Love*, readers are less a theater audience than peep show patrons, and what we see is an unrelieved spectacle of pain and suffering. The triangle of Lee, Annabel, and Buzz hermetically excludes all others, and *Love* itself mirrors this exclusion. Unlike *Several Perceptions*, in which the language points to myriad interpretive levels and thus draws the reader into the text through the act of interpretation, *Love* distances the reader. Like Buzz, the reader is a voyeur, and because the affect in *Love* is remarkably flat, it is easy to watch the spectacle passively, despite its strangeness. Even Annabel's suicide attempt is described with all the emotional intensity of pouring tea: "She went immediately to the bathroom to kill herself in private. Fortunately it was unoccupied" (*Love*, 45).

Every spectacle, however disturbing, needs an audience to watch it. To look is to have power, and the dominant, direct gaze is most often a male prerogative. Men look; women are looked at. Buzz's camera obsession is a good example of this because looking, for him, is a way of gaining power: it reduces complexities to surfaces. His looking turns the subjects of his look into objects. Annabel has "visionary eyes" (*Love*, 17), which Lee feels might pierce "his disarming crust of charm to find beneath it some other person who was, perhaps, himself" (*Love*, 17), but he is fooling himself in thinking that her eyes might plumb the truthful depths of his soul. Annabel's gaze is vampiric, and by looking at Lee, she drains from him his own sense of himself: "Over the years, she drew and painted him again and again in so many different disguises that at last he had to go to another woman to find out the true likeness of his face" (*Love*, 25). As in the beating, Annabel reverses the usual male/female distinction. Her eyes are her most distinctive feature, and she takes an active role in looking. Of the three characters, Lee is the only one who is unable to look at anyone directly. It is a nice correlation to his false sentimentality that he sees through a veil of tears caused not by emotion but by an infection that produces photophobia. His tears allow him a hypocritical advantage because they are seen by the women with whom he has affairs as evidence of his sensitivity.

The Logic of Unreason

Communication between Buzz, Annabel, and Lee is desultory at best. In place of linguistic communication, they leave their marks on each other's bodies in bruises. Lee feels an "unspoken contact with [Annabel], like that of two people from different countries who do not speak one another's language thrust together in a third whose language neither understands" (*Love*, 17). His metaphor is more appropriate than the conclusions he draws from it. If one assumes that love requires some mutual appreciation of thought, experience, or interest, then Carter's title is savagely ironic. Buzz and Lee have brief, factual, or histrionic exchanges when they are not physically battling one another. Buzz and

Annabel "play inscrutable games together" (*Love*, 44), and even in her moments of distress or as she is lying in the blood from her slashed wrists, she is, for Buzz, a photographic opportunity. Each character, indeed, has a vampiric relation to the others, and any weakness is exploited as an opportunity to wound. When Lee is forced to expel Buzz from their home after Annabel's suicide attempt, he does so because Annabel now defines Lee as having "no life beyond that of a necessary attribute of herself alone" (*Love*, 64). He is now her victim, and her power over him means that she can "change him in any way she please[s]" (*Love*, 71).

Annabel's suicide attempt is a punishment for Lee's infidelity; her final, successful, attempt is a peculiar form of mastery over herself. Between the two, she tries to gain greater autonomy than she has had thus far, and her first action is cleverly contrived to turn Lee's sentimentalism against him by making it literal. She takes him to a tattooist and forces him to have a heart and her name (in Gothic script) inscribed on his chest. Having signed him as one of her possessions, she feels, he will no longer be able to be unfaithful. She takes a number of jobs, including one at a local ballroom, and her success is due to her having counterfeited Lee's only spontaneous smile. When Buzz reappears, their torture of Lee reaches its peak as Buzz kisses Annabel in a public bar in front of Lee and their friends, and Buzz and Annabel leave together to engage in what will be Annabel's undoing. Her fantasies of Buzz have been an attempt "to convince herself she [is] alive," but when reality fails her, first with Buzz and later in the "mutual rape" with Lee, there is no alternative in her "remorseless logic of unreason" but to die (*Love*, 95–101). Before she does, though, she remakes herself as a spectacle for display, her own artistic creation, "her own, omnipotent white queen" (*Love*, 104).

The most disturbing aspect of this sad drama is that the culmination of Annabel's autonomy is to take her own life. Self-immolation is hardly a triumph, but the power Annabel feels in preparing for her death, although illusory, is the only power available to her. She has been a commodity for Lee, a role that is underlined by the economic metaphors he consistently uses to describe how he feels for her. His response to her transformation is, on one hand, to invoke revolutionary language—"*Le jour de gloire est arrivé*" (*Love*, 104)—but, on the other, to see her difference as creating his bankruptcy, "for there was nothing left for him to love" (*Love*, 104). Nonetheless, the rupture that Annabel's life and death have caused is only a temporary loss of capital. The brothers come together at her death, reinvesting in their old squabbles, "for nothing but death is irreparable" (*Love*, 112).

Afterword

Carter wrote *Love* in 1969 and revised it in 1987. To the revised edition, she appended an afterword in which she comments on the novel and updates the lives of the characters. She describes *Love* as an "almost sinister feat of male impersonation" (*Love*, 114), but there is a continued feat of impersonation here: the author as biographer. Although Carter is ostensibly writing as herself, the afterword is certainly part of the novel, even though it provides an illusion of biographical reality, as if the characters had somehow stepped out of the novel to share the reader's ontology. Given that Carter is clearly turning her 1987 postmodernist eye on her more naturalistic 1969 novel, the reality effect is clearly a ruse, despite the narrative insistence that the characters' portraits are indeed "real life" (*Love*, 116). Here, as in a good deal of her fiction from the later period, she is using the conventions of literary realism only to undermine them. Particularly evident in this regard is the clarity of the narrative voice: despite Carter's sly insistence on the characters' autonomy, the narrative voice is so overtly insistent that this is clearly not a slice of life. The characters portrayed in the afterword are as much fictional creations as they were in the novel proper, and this technique gives readers a taste of the playful narrative strategies that Carter will use in her later fiction.

Chapter Four

Eves at the End of the World:
The Magic Toyshop and
Heroes and Villains

Toward the end of *Heroes and Villains* (1969), Jewel exhorts Marianne to pretend she is "Eve at the end of the world,"[1] a situation that describes the predicament of the female heroes in both novels discussed in this chapter. Marianne leaves the safe, if static, world of her childhood home by choice; Melanie, in *The Magic Toyshop* (1967), is forced from both childhood and home by her parents' deaths. Though both young women have imagined the world outside the gates of their symbolic Edens, neither is prepared for what she finds there. Both are suddenly thrust into settings where they have to fight to establish adult identities against those who would turn them into puppets. The threshold of a new life is a place of both excitement and terror, and because neither Marianne nor Melanie can return home, they are forced to cope by drawing on their own resources. Although each woman is subjected to violence, neither is overwhelmed by it. Unlike the women in the Bristol Trilogy, neither Marianne nor Melanie chooses helplessness or masochism as appropriate behaviors. Both novels seem to suggest a more active method of dealing with oppression than was available to Ghislaine or Annabel, and that method is to fight back with a strong sense of self.

The Magic Toyshop is about the obsessive creation of a fantasy world; *Heroes and Villains* speculates about the power of myth in a postapocalyptic landscape. These novels represent Carter's first forays into speculative fiction, the genre with which she is most popularly identified. In *Fantasy: The Literature of Subversion,* Rosemary Jackson argues that fantasy "attempts to compensate for a lack resulting from cultural constraints,"[2] and although this is certainly true of Carter's speculative fictions, it is important to point out that her fantasy worlds are not idealized. Many are dystopias in which violence, cruelty, and manipulation are commonplace. Like the Gothic novels whose conventions she

uses frequently, Carter's fantasy worlds are dark, brooding, and dangerous, and these are the very qualities that their female heroes often find
so attractive. Few of Carter's women characters after the Bristol Trilogy
succumb to helplessness; rather, they are "wayward girls and wicked
women." They have strong wills and animal natures, and they do assert
themselves most forcefully. This, perhaps, is how these novels most
obviously overturn cultural constraints.

The Magic Toyshop

The Magic Toyshop is narrated in the third person from the perspective of
15-year-old Melanie. When her wealthy parents are killed in a plane
crash while traveling in America, her comfortable world comes to an
end. Melanie and her younger siblings, Jonathon and Victoria, are sent
from their country home to live with their Uncle Philip in South London. Philip is a clever toy maker with a passion for life-size puppets. He
is also a miserly and tyrannical patriarch who controls every aspect of his
household. Philip appears seldom in the novel and speaks only to utter
criticism, issue orders, or narrate his puppet shows; however, his presence fills the house, and his dependents learn to police themselves in
response to his absolute rules. Philip's Irish wife, Margaret, is a desic-
cated woman who was struck dumb on her wedding day and communicates by means of chalkboards and writing pads. Like Melanie, Margaret
is an orphan, and the novel suggests that her marriage to Philip is a
means to provide a home for her brothers, Francie and Finn Jowles.
Gentle Francie is the least affected by Philip's tyranny because he has
some small means of economic independence in playing his fiddle. Finn
is the toy maker's apprentice and a talented painter, but he courts
Philip's irrational violence with his insolence and is beaten because of it.
When Finn tears the controls from one of Philip's puppets during a performance, Philip throws Finn from the flies and he crashes onto the
stage. This is the beginning of outright war between the two, and it precipitates Philip's plan to have Melanie act with one of the puppets in a
performance of "Leda and the Swan." Although he barely acknowledges
the children's presence in his house, forcing Melanie into the role of
Leda is Philip's revenge on their dead father. He instructs Finn to
rehearse Melanie for the role, hoping, as Finn sees it, that her figurative
rape will be preceded by a real one. Melanie's father was a writer and
represents, for Philip, the enemy "who use[s] toilet paper and fish

knives."[3] To defile the children is to win a battle in a war between the classes, and by making Melanie play Leda, Philip is trying to control her as he does his puppets.

People, indeed, hardly matter at all to Philip, except as they obey or disobey his rules. His kindnesses are directed solely to his puppets, and the house has few amenities for its human occupants. Having recently discovered and delighted in her developing body, Melanie finds the discomfort particularly difficult. There is no pleasure in the house except when Philip is away and the Jowleses celebrate with music and dancing. Jonathon is lost to Melanie early on because his passion for building model ships puts him firmly in Philip's grasp. Victoria is five, although her behavior is that of a baby, and she is soon being looked after by Margaret. Melanie eventually enters the Jowleses' loving circle, although she has ambivalent feelings for Finn. She is repelled by his smell and dirty clothes and thinks him common. But Finn has a talent for allegory and romanticism, as she discovers when he takes her to the ruins of the 1852 National Exhibition. Although he can paint "in the manner of a Rubens allegory" (*MT*, 99), quote Shelley, and understand the despair that accompanies the "graveyard of a pleasure ground" (*MT*, 101), he is far from being the romantic hero of her fantasies. When he kisses her against her will she is horrified, although proximity soon makes her think she might be in love with him.

It is Finn, however, who finally takes the heroic action that will lead to liberation from Philip's tyranny. After the performance of "Leda and the Swan," Finn steals the swan puppet, chops it up, and buries it in the exhibition grounds. His daring action is partly suicidal. He has been courting Philip's "killing blow" (*MT*, 135), on the grounds that his murder will damn Philip, and destroying the swan seems a likely way for Finn to get his wish. He is also protecting Melanie: "I did it partly for your sake, because it [the swan] rode you" (*MT*, 174). The celebration that follows Finn's liberating disobedience is made more jolly by Philip's absence. Everything is turned upside down, and a carnival spirit reigns: Finn takes a bath, Melanie dons trousers (forbidden by Philip), Margaret is transformed by wearing Melanie's dress and pearls, Guinness flows, and music fills the house. In the midst of all the merriment, Francie and Margaret embrace, and Melanie discovers that they are, and always have been, lovers. Unfortunately, Philip returns to find brother and sister in each other's arms and with insane glee vows to "trap them like rats and burn them out!" (*MT*, 197). Margaret, her voice recovered, urges Finn to flee with Melanie, and the two escape through a skylight.

The novel ends with the house in flames, and Finn and Melanie staring at each other in a neglected garden.

Sexual Bodies

The novel opens with Melanie's exploration of her body as an uncharted landscape. Although she spends hours in narcissistic contemplation, there is nonetheless something delightfully unselfconscious about her overwhelming joy in the "supple surprise of herself now she was no longer a little girl" (*MT*, 1). She tries out her new body in various poses drawn from paintings, she puts forget-me-nots in her pubic hair after reading *Lady Chatterly's Lover,* and she constructs fantasies of a phantom bridegroom that are so intense that she can "almost feel his breath on her cheek" (*MT*, 2). Sitting in church, she prays that she will be married, or at least have sex, and she worries that she has already passed her prime. Melanie has company for her fantasizing. Even the housekeeper, the prosaic Mrs. Rundle, remembers a husband she never had, and Jonathon, who is only barely conscious of the world around him, "rove[s] uncharted seas" (*MT*, 4) in imagined ships.

Melanie oversteps the bounds of her innocent idyll, however, on the night she enters her absent parents' bedroom. As an almost fairy-tale foreshadowing of what is to come, Melanie sees Uncle Philip in her parents' wedding photo and is reminded of the jack-in-the-box he once sent her from which a "grotesque parody of her own face" (*MT*, 12) jumped out. This presages Melanie's future, in which she will lose her own mirrored face to various parodies of it constructed by her uncle. Philip's manipulations, however, are different only in degree from the ones to which Melanie has already subjected herself. Although she chooses to pose in front of the mirror as a kind of live art, she has a limited choice of female roles on which to draw. Despite the joyful tone of her self-discovery, she is still constrained by social and artistic perceptions of what a sexual woman can be: a Toulouse-Lautrec bawd or a Cranach Venus (*MT*, 1–2). The wedding photo leads Melanie to speculate about her mother's sexuality, the symbolism of the white dress, and the letters Melanie has read in women's magazines about premarital relations. Implicit in Melanie's speculations is a sense that there are rules for women's sexual deportment that have little to do with the kind of playfulness she has exhibited in front of the mirror.

Melanie's fall from grace begins when she tries on her mother's wedding dress, in which she is "sufficient for herself in her own glory and

[does] not need a groom" (*MT*, 16). She wanders out into the night, but the vast loneliness of the sky fills her with terror, and nature seems to turn against her. Finding herself locked out of the house, she takes off the dress, already stained with blood from her cut feet, and climbs the apple tree to her own room. In the apple tree, she suddenly becomes conscious of her nakedness, and because the imagery is clearly that of Genesis, her disobedience is placed on a grand scale. Having stained the wedding dress and ripped it to shreds, she has symbolically lost the innocence that led her to think she was autonomous. Symbolically, in trying on the wedding dress, she has tried on her mother's sexuality, and neither of them fits her. Melanie has tried on "too much, too soon" (*MT*, 18). In figurative terms, wearing the dress usurps her mother's position as the sexual woman in the family. This exciting infraction, however, makes Melanie think that she has literally killed her mother by symbolically replacing her, and when the telegram comes the next day, Melanie doesn't have to read it to know what it says. She is convinced that by wearing the dress, she has caused her parents' deaths. The wedding dress is a symbol of virginity and of initiation into sexuality. Discovering herself as a sexual being, however, is also a discovery of shame, and for this Melanie feels that she is punished by losing her parents. In her grief, she smashes her mirror and then wrecks her parents' bedroom "like an automaton" (*MT*, 25). When Mrs. Rundle finds Melanie, she has covered her face with her mother's crimson lipstick and black mascara as visible evidence of her sexuality as a wound.[4]

Melanie's ability to delight in her body is partly a result of her class. In her parents' house, she has the leisure and the means to be comfortable with her self-regard. Once she moves to her uncle's home, however, her body is a register of comparative poverty. She cannot keep it clean or warm, and she feels she has lost control of it. Putting away the cutlery one day, she feels she is a "wind-up putting-away doll, clicking through its programmed movements" (*MT*, 76). Not only is she watched by Finn through a peephole between their bedrooms, but she feels as though her uncle's "colourless eyes were judging and assessing her all the time" (*MT*, 92). Philip also dictates her manner of dress. He thinks that a woman wearing trousers is a "harlot" (*MT*, 62), and he forbids makeup.

Philip's parsimony and misogyny similarly control Margaret's clothing. Her skirts and sweaters are in tatters, and her stockings are in ruin. Only on Sundays does she dress in her best clothes, and even they are dowdy. The crowning glory of her Sunday costume is a silver collar that rises almost to her chin and forces her to keep her head unnaturally erect. Her wedding present from Philip, who made it himself, the collar is uncomfortable and prevents her from eating, while her husband derives a "certain pleasure from her discomfort" (*MT*, 113). Bodily discomfort and humiliation is the price Melanie and Margaret pay for having a roof over their heads. They are "poor women pensioners, planets round a male sun" (*MT*, 140).

On the wedding-dress night, Melanie enacts her desires, and the consequences are tragic. Exhibiting herself, even if only to the sky, is as transgressive an act as usurping her mother's place. But the power she feels in unleashing her desires is extraordinary, delightful, and terrifying. From the moment she enters her uncle's house, however, she passively accepts the strictures he imposes, including not going to school. Despite not wanting to play Leda in her uncle's puppet show, her response is simply "needs must" (*MT*, 141). Only when she is faced with the possibility of a real sexual relationship with Finn does she revolt. Finn's kiss in the ruined pleasure garden is humiliating, "a rude encroachment on her physical privacy" (*MT*, 106). Once again, she wishes for a fantasy to combat her lack of desire: "She wished someone was watching them, to appreciate them, or that she herself was watching them, Finn kissing this black-haired young girl, from a bush a hundred yards away. Then it would seem romantic" (*MT*, 106).

Melanie uses cinematic imagery as she has used painting and literature in order to find a model for her behavior and a language with which to communicate.[5] She uses film as a way of dealing with her situation, partly because film appeals to her sense of the dramatic, but also because sitting in a theater is ordinary and temporary. When she is feeling particularly alone and miserable in her uncle's house, she fantasizes that someone might soon appear selling popcorn, and this fantasy is a rather poignant indication of her hope that Philip and the strangeness he represents might well disappear as the credits role. In the scene with Finn in the ruined pleasure garden, she thinks that she and Finn must look like a shot from "a new-wave British film" (*MT*, 106). She deals with Philip by seeing him as an actor, possibly Orson Welles, and she yearns to break into the Jowleses' "home movie" (*MT*, 76). She comments that watching a film is "like being a voyeur, living vicariously" (*MT*, 76), and this explains her narrative detachment from her surroundings. She is more comfortable in a world of romantic fantasy because this has been her only option. Even when she thinks she might be falling in love with Finn, who has so far disgusted her because of his very unromantic smell, "terrifying maleness" (*MT*, 45), and "common" (*MT*, 77) manners, she has no language with which to tell him. Her attempt to do so prompts Finn's accusation that she sounds "like a woman's magazine" (*MT*, 155).

From the first morning in her uncle's house, Melanie feels "insecure in her own personality" (*MT*, 58). Her grief at losing her parents and her home certainly contribute to this insecurity, but so does a radical change in the fantasies available to her. She does not recognize herself in her new home; first, because it exhibits the trappings of a different class, and second, because the images she is given there are those of a clear subordination to which she is not accustomed. Finn's portrait of her, though "flat and uncommunicative" (*MT*, 153), presents her as a freshly scrubbed virgin. Although the portrait is perhaps a more faithful rendition of Melanie than some of the poses she has chosen for herself, it is still "an asexual kind of pin-up" (*MT*, 154), and misses the struggle she is having with herself as a sexual being. On the threshold of sexuality, Melanie finds few ways of expressing it, although the images offered to her in her uncle's house strangely mirror the ones she once tried out for herself in her bedroom. No longer Cranach or Toulouse-Lautrec, her choices are now Leda or asexual self. The source of the images has changed, but their message has not.

Puppet Bodies

In Carter's story "The Loves of Lady Purple," a puppet comes to life; in *The Magic Toyshop*, life is subservient to the puppets. Nonetheless, Carter's description of the puppet master is appropriate: "The puppeteer speculates in a no-man's-limbo between the real and that which, although we know very well it is not, nevertheless seems to be real."[6] Philip Flower's magic toy shop exemplifies precisely this limbo, but because the confusion between the real and the not real happens not on a stage but in the "ordinary" world, it is particularly sinister.

Philip's toys are uncannily realistic; even Finn admits that Philip is a genius in his craft. The toys, however are hardly playthings. They are representations and interpretations of Philip's world, and all are evidence of his desire for control. Through his toys and puppets, he parodies life and art. For Melanie, the simulacrum is too much: "This crazy world whirled about her, men and women dwarfed by toys and puppets, where even the birds were mechanical and the few human figures went masked" (*MT*, 68). There are no mirrors in the house because the toys come to represent the occupants. Looking at one's own face in a mirror is a manner of self-recognition, and Philip wants his family to be mirrored only in his perceptions of them. In this, he has clearly succeeded; the extent to which the inhabitants of Philip's house will go to support his obsession is astonishing. Everything in the house whirls around him, even when he is absent from it. His power is largely economic. Although there is plenty of food, Philip allows his family few other comforts. There is no hot water, no toilet paper, and little heat. Household items are bought on credit; thus no one in the house has money. Fear of Philip's irrational and erratic violence keeps everyone in line, although it is Finn who suffers most frequently from Philip's actual blows.

As Melanie has discovered, confusing reality and fantasy can be a dangerous pursuit. In her new home, she is thrust into a similar confusion, although not one of her own making. Not only are the toys and puppets uncannily real, but everything in and around Philip's house seems to have a life of its own. The wallpaper seems to grow thorns, the hot water geyser is maniacal, and Philip's chair is ominous. Melanie feels she has entered Bluebeard's castle, and that having "married the shadows" (*MT*, 77) on the wedding-dress night, she is, like Bluebeard's wives, faced with a house full of sinister rooms. So real does this image become to her that she hallucinates a young girl's severed hand in a cutlery drawer. Francie, who finds Melanie after she faints at the gory sight, suggests that the distress of her loss might make her imagine such things. Not only has she lost her parents and her home, but her brother Jonathon is lost to Philip, as is her sister Victoria to Margaret. Left only with responsibility for herself, even Melanie's body seems to erode and fall apart; certainly her delight in her body has vanished. Like Melanie's description of herself as a doll without volition (*MT*, 76), the severed hand aligns her with what she sees in Philip's workshop, a "*Walpurgisnacht* of carved and severed limbs" (*MT*, 66).

Paulina Palmer writes that Carter uses the image of the puppet to "represent women's role in society" and to suggest the manner in which "human beings are reduced by a process of psychic repression."[7] Because Melanie's discovery of sexual autonomy is, in her eyes, the cause of expulsion from her Edenic past, it is not surprising that part of what she sees as her punishment should be the loss of that autonomy. The puppet master's world is a world in limbo, but Melanie is in a similar, in-between state. Too young and too small for some things, she is too big and too old for others. Finn makes much of Melanie's being too young for a sexual relationship (*MT*, 151, 153), as she was too young and too small for the wedding dress and all that it represented. In Philip's house, everyone is diminished by his enormous bulk, and Melanie wonders whether she will wither as Margaret has. Not having a mirror, Melanie sees herself reflected "in little" (*MT*, 105) in Finn's eyes, and in approaching her performance as Leda, she feels powerless in a world carrying her, "infinitely small, furious, reluctant, with it" (*MT*, 162). Although Philip wishes to make his nephew and nieces into "little Flowers" (*MT*, 144), Melanie is not small enough for his ideal Leda: "I wanted my Leda to be a little girl. Your tits are too big" (*MT*, 143).

Melanie is no longer in control of the sight of her own body; the world she has entered watches her, judges her, and determines how she sees herself. Although this is couched in the terms of a fairy-tale fantasy, complete with motifs such as the wicked uncle, orphaned children, mute woman, and isolation, as well as a disturbing blend of the real and the unreal, what happens to Melanie is hardly confined to fairy tales. Although her uncle's toy shop seems alien and sinister, it provides an education in female behavior and sexuality that is, unfortunately, quite ordinary.

Leda

The culmination of Philip's control comes when he forces Melanie to play the role of Leda to his huge puppet swan. Philip seems to have a peculiar clairvoyance when it comes to Melanie's inner life. This fairy-tale element creates an atmosphere of dread, especially when Melanie begins to notice images from the wedding-dress night appearing in Philip's house. A music box in the shape of a white rose, whose petals open to reveal a tiny, dancing shepherdess, and a black-haired puppet dressed in white tulle remind Melanie of her adventure in the moonlight. The costume for her portrayal of Leda is diaphanous white chiffon of the kind Melanie once used to put on in front of her mirror: "Melanie would be a nymph crowned with daisies once again; he saw her as once she had seen herself. In spite of everything, she was flattered" (*MT*, 141).

The puppet shows are some of the weirder events in the novel. Here, as everywhere else, Philip's authority is maintained, if not lauded, by his family, although there is something pathetic about the formality of the show and the family's forced appreciation. Philip puts on his puppet shows as though to a large crowd, although the family is his only audience. Unwritten rules dictate that they applaud wildly and throw paper roses. If Melanie has not already been schooled in the contradiction between her imagined romantic fantasies and the reality of her subordination, the performance in which she plays Leda makes it explicit. The structure of the show imitates that of the wedding-dress night. Melanie is once again clothed in a costume whose purpose is to draw attention to sexuality. The shells on the stage cut her feet, and she is overwhelmed by the horror of her position: "she felt herself not herself, wrenched from her own personality" (*MT*, 166). She feels she must perform well or be savaged by "an armed host of pigmy Uncle Philips" (*MT*, 166) that might rush from the belly of the swan. At first, the swan seems "dumpy and homely" (*MT*, 165), but as it covers her, its obscenity becomes overwhelming, and Melanie loses consciousness. Philip's savagery in mounting this performance is compounded by his smacking Melanie for overacting and spoiling the poetry. Having forced her to act like a puppet, he is offended that she is not one.

Although Finn is hardly Melanie's ideal romantic hero, and she is terrified of the kind of life he seems to offer her—"babies crying and washing to be done and toast burning all the rest of her life" (*MT*, 177)—he does rush to her rescue by dismembering and burying the swan. Killing the swan symbolizes killing Philip, and the atmosphere in the house the next day is one of celebration and liberation from his tyranny. In the Greek myth, Leda is raped by Zeus, but produces two sets of offspring. Pollux and Helen are fathered by Zeus; Clytemnestra and Castor by Leda's husband, Tyndareus. This coupling is not only a rape; it leads, through the progeny who result from it, to terrible tragedy: Helen's adultery causes the Trojan War, and Clytemnestra's adultery leads to the death of her husband, Agamemnon, upon his return from the Trojan War. The performance of "Leda and the Swan" also produces tragedy, if on a more domestic scale: Philip discovers the incestuous love between Margaret and Francie; the house is burned down, and all but Finn and Melanie seem to be burned with it.

Despite the fantasy element in the novel, Melanie learns some very ordinary lessons about what life as a woman has to offer. The course of the novel is a slow erosion of Melanie's delight as she becomes dependent, manipulated, and victimized. Unlike her predecessor Ghislaine, or the other women in the Bristol Trilogy, however, Melanie does not choose masochism as a response. She seeks friendship from Margaret and community from Finn and Francie, and although she does not take an active role in protesting her position, she does not, at least, succumb to self-obliteration.

The novel's ending is ambiguous. The "wild surmise" (*MT*, 200) with which Melanie and Finn face each other is in light of the death of the puppet master, but like Adam and Eve, Melanie and Finn find themselves in a ruined garden. Lorna Sage comments that Melanie "learns to dream prophetically,"[8] and that she rescues her brother from the fire by dreaming him out of it and onto one of his ships. Her other "prophetic vision" (*MT*, 177), however, is of her life with Finn, surrounded by squalor and crying babies, and in this context, her newfound freedom seems yet another entrapment.

Heroes and Villains

Heroes and Villains takes place after what seems to have been a global conflagration. In an effort to preserve the icons, knowledge, and structures of prewar civilization, Professors were protected in underground bunkers in the hope that they would emerge to "resurrect the gone world in a gentler shape" (*HV*, 8). The technology that would have given rise to this destruction seems to have disappeared, but the structure of the new world is still based on antagonism between the Professors and the remaining people who have managed to survive. The Barbarians, who live outside the Professors' guarded enclave, are nomadic hunters and scavengers who are prey to disease, malnutrition, and early death. Whereas the Professors are little more than museum pieces living protected and comfortable lives, the Barbarians have had to learn to survive in a chaotic, contaminated landscape. They are superstitious and savage, and what they cannot procure for themselves they steal from the Professors in dangerous raids. On one of these raids, Marianne, the daughter of a Professor of History, watches as her brother is slain by a Barbarian boy whose face comes to haunt her dreams.

Even as a child, Marianne is tough, resilient, and angry. Most important, she is a skeptic who looks at the world with a cool, bemused eye. When her father is murdered by her old nurse, Marianne no longer feels any ties to her home, and she escapes with the Barbarian named Jewel, who has hidden from the soldiers during a raid. Jewel is a beautiful, exotic boy who has been educated, though kept illiterate, by his tutor Donally, a renegade Professor who has set himself up as the resident shaman. Donally maintains his authority by virtue of a chest of poisons and a viper he keeps in a box. The Barbarians live in a ruined house, and if Donally's role is presiding father, the maternal element is provided by Mrs. Green, Jewel's foster mother. She attempts to protect Marianne from Donally's poisons, from the fear she engenders in members of the community, and from an attempted gang rape by Jewel's brothers. Seeing the danger of her position as an outsider, and therefore as a focus for all the resentments and superstitions of the Barbarians, Marianne decides to escape. She is tracked, raped, and returned, however, by Jewel and is forced to marry him in a ceremony combining the Book of Common Prayer with a ritual bloodletting.

Marianne learns sexual desire from Jewel, although they reenact, both in the bedroom and out of it, their social and personal antagonisms. In the Barbarian community, Marianne feels the power of her anger as self-protection. On her wedding night, she begins to enjoy herself when Jewel starts to radiate fear and anger, a result of his sudden recognition that she once watched him kill her brother and that now she will be the death of him. Convinced that Marianne will take revenge on him, that she is "biding her time till the fatal moment" (*HV*, 122), Jewel finds his own revenge in making her pregnant. This too is an act of war: "Shoving a little me up you, a little me all furred, plaited and bristling with knives" (*HV*, 90). For Marianne, pleasure dies when it is "ancillary to procreation" (*HV*, 91), and she accuses Jewel of wishing to humiliate her by making her "give birth to monsters" (*HV*, 90).

Her pregnancy terrifies her and causes her a brief moment of vulnerability in which she clings to Jewel. In a conversation that follows the revelation of her pregnancy, Donally urges Jewel to accept his responsibilities. Donally wants to make Jewel into a messianic figure, a mythically inspired hero who will conquer the world with terror. Jewel has no place to which he can escape from the fate Donally proposes. When Jewel thinks of turning himself over to the Professors, Marianne warns him that to them, he will be nothing more than an exotic exhibit or a laboratory specimen. Instead, Jewel decides to banish Donally, a move that Marianne fears will arouse even more superstitious fears among the Barbarians.

Throughout the novel, Jewel's mood swings from anger to melancholy as he waits for Marianne to exact her revenge. In the wake of Donally's parting, Jewel tries to drown himself in the sea, although Marianne, as she has done twice before, saves his life. When a note comes from Donally with the words "save me" written on it, Jewel and his brothers form a rescue party. Before they leave, Marianne makes an odd gesture in telling him that she "did not even love [her] brother much" (*HV*, 148). On the one hand, this information, though an affront to Jewel's own familial affections, diminishes her threat to him. But on the other, it robs him of the anger that combats his melancholy. When he dies, shot by a soldier who may simply have been out shooting pigeons, it is a death without heroism. Marianne is left to fend for herself, vowing that she will take on the role Donally wished for Jewel, to rule the Barbarians "with a rod of iron" (*HV*, 150).

The Fall of the Noble Savage

The art of the Professors is knowledge of the past, although what they seek to preserve is already anachronistic. Because they are cut off from the world beyond their fortresses, the Professors' knowledge is inured against any change that might come from interaction with the present. Even the language of the past is rapidly losing its meaning; Marianne cannot respond to her father's question about the meaning of the word "city" (*HV*, 7), and dictionaries point to concepts that no longer have a recognizable context: "these words had ceased to describe facts and now stood only for ideas or memories" (*HV*, 7). The Professors' knowledge is now no different from the superstitions propounded by Marianne's nurse, and later by the Barbarians. The intellectual elite are a dying breed, and their knowledge, because it cannot be disseminated in the larger world, will die with them. If remembered at all, it will be as ancient mythologies from an unknowable past.

The aim of a dystopian novel such as *Heroes and Villains* is to encourage readers to see the similarities between our own world and the fictional one. This aim is didactic in that it seeks to warn readers of attitudes, behaviors, and conventional ideas that might lead to the catastrophes adumbrated in the fiction. In the context of the novel, the knowledge of the Professors seems useless because it is knowledge without utility and without moral aim. Carter is clearly not disavowing knowledge itself here; her own writing consistently celebrates and rewards the bibliophile. The novel does raise questions about how knowledge is used, and whether it is used to oppress people. For example, Marianne's father has a theory about the Barbarians that mimics apartheid. For him, they serve a necessary function as scapegoats, but he believes that they would destroy the world if they ever gained control of it. The Professors worship reason, but because reason has little to say to Barbarians struggling for food and against disease, the two groups cannot communicate.

Carter commented in an interview that *Heroes and Villains* is "a discussion of the theories of Jean-Jacques Rousseau, and strangely enough it finds them wanting."[9] Marianne's father tells her that "Rousseau spoke of a noble savage, but this is a time of ignoble savages" (*HV*, 10). Because there is little nobility in disease and starvation, his statement would seem to indicate that Rousseau would be unable to understand the world inhabited by these Barbarians. In such a setting, there is little place for Rousseau's notion that essential human goodness can exist only in a state of nature. The novel juxtaposes this idea with the biblical precept of original sin. Neither myth is given precedence; the novel raises the conflicting ideas of human goodness and evil without resolving them. In the act of reading and apprehending traces of a distant fictional past, the reader is being asked to consider not only these specific contentions but, more generally, how knowledge gains the status of truth.

Donally takes advantage of his superior education to create a selective mythology for the Barbarians. Unlike the Professors, Donally has used his knowledge to attempt to create a social system, although he is a tyrant who plays on superstitious fears to achieve his ends. On the brink of exile, he warns that his departure will bring about the end of art, culture, wit, and humor, for like the Professors, Donally has kept all of these largely to himself. Although he has taught Jewel enough to participate in intellectual debate, Donally has refused to teach Jewel to read and write, so as to "maintain him in a crude state of unrefined energy" (*HV*, 62). In essence, Donally has had to teach Jewel to become the noble savage, although what Donally himself seems to believe in more readily is the biblical notion of human evil. Through fear, Donally hopes to craft a new religion: "coaxed from incoherence, we shall leave the indecent condition of barbarism and aspire to that of honest savage" (*HV*, 63).

On Jewel's back, Donally has tattooed an elaborate picture of Eve offering the apple to Adam. Tattooing, Donally says, "is the first of the post-apocalyptic arts, its materials are flesh and blood" (*HV*, 125). The tableau is meant to be a reminder of the consequences of gaining the knowledge of good and evil, although it is significant that Jewel himself cannot see the picture. Given the importance of this particular moment within the myth of the Fall in Western culture, it is tempting to try to draw correspondences between it and the novel. Marianne, for example, is associated with Eve, as Donally, with his serpent in a box, is connected to Satan. The particular temptation of knowledge, however, leads only to more questions. *Heroes and Villains* represents an already fallen world, and there is no suggestion that a paradise existed in the past or awaits in the future: there is none of Rousseau's optimism with regard to the savage's state of natural grace. Indeed, the tableau is a reminder that original innocence is lost and irretrievable. Marianne brings death to the community only in the sense that she is blamed for all inexplicable tragedy. For Jewel, she is the personification of his doom because he expects her to exact an Old Testament retribution, avenging her brother's death. Marianne's belief in reason is out of place in the Barbarian's superstitious world, and while she is therefore unpredictable to them, she is hardly the purveyor of the end of paradise. Nor is she an Eve who would willingly share her apple with any Adam. The pieces of the puzzle do not fit neatly because their exact correspondences are less important than the broad relationship between past and present knowledge, including the consequences of the loss of history in a world whose surviving documents are fragmented and anachronistic.

Object of Desire

In the absence of literacy, Donally works in visual images. Tattoos adorn most of the Barbarians, but the tableau on Jewel's back is Donally's masterpiece. The materiality of postapocalyptic arts of the body contrasts the Professors' devotion to the ethereal mind, although tattooing is an art that is also torture. The pain Donally inflicts in the process is sadistic, and the finished product on Jewel's back arouses Donally's desires. Jewel tells Marianne that he was delirious with pain for two weeks, and that a girl whom Donally tried to tattoo with tiger stripes died. Despite Marianne's fascination with the tattoo, she calls it a mutilation, and in her eyes, Jewel takes on "the ghastly attraction of the deformed" (*HV*, 86). Because it is drawn on his skin, Jewel's tattoo exists at the surface between self and other, blurring the distinction between social and private selves. Marianne comments that Jewel can never be completely naked or completely alone, because Adam and Eve are always there. His body ceases to be his own, becoming instead the gallery of Donally's talent, which he "prowls round admiring" (*HV*, 86). Although Jewel's tattoo (which he cannot see) does not itself make him into an artifact, it does emphasize his status as an object. With his beautiful face, long hair, necklaces, and adorned body, Jewel is very much a feminized figure. In a society whose cultural memory is discontinuous, gender roles are not fixed. Marianne exercises the stereotypically male attributes of reason and logic. She is fearless and strong willed, and when he first meets her, Jewel thinks she is a boy because of her short hair.

At the beginning of the novel, the children in the enclave play "heroes and villains," a game whose rules dictate that the Soldiers (who protect the Professors) will always triumph over the Barbarians. When the son of the Professor of Mathematics says he is a hero and will shoot her, Marianne refuses to play, but she does leave the boy sprawled in the dust. With similar self-possession, Marianne refuses all mythologies that attempt to objectify her. She gets angry when she becomes the source of superstitious fear, and she refuses Donally's offer to teach her necromancy because, she says, it doesn't work. Despite Jewel's refusal of Donally's plans to make him a messiah, Jewel is more pliant and more passive than Marianne. When he recognizes her as the "severe child" (*HV*, 6) who looked at the spectacle of the Barbarian raid as though it were "all an entertainment laid on for her benefit" (*HV*, 80), he gives himself up to fatalism. From that moment on, he is consumed by the imagery of death. When he looks at Marianne, he imagines her as death wearing black gloves or as a firing squad. "It's fatal, fear of death" (*HV*, 29), he says to Marianne, and so it proves to be for him. His passive acceptance of what he construes as his fate contrasts with Marianne's skepticism. Despite everything that happens to her, she is determined to survive. The instability of gender markings, however, does not change the materiality of biology. At the sexual level, Marianne is victimized as a woman, although she refuses to allow violence to deny her autonomy.

Object of Violence

When Jewel's brothers attempt to subdue Marianne through rape, they do so after a scene in which they cut up the kill of the day for distribution. The kitchen and the men are awash in blood. The attempted rape is presented as an extension of the violence of the kill and the apportioning of food. Marianne's is the next body to be divvied up, and she is treated as though she is indistinguishable from the other carcasses. When she pretends she does not exist, it is because, for her would-be violators, she does not. She is saved by Donally, who comments ironically on the brothers' bravery by saying that it is a well-known fact that the Professor women "sprout sharp teeth in their private parts to bite off the genitalia of young men" (*HV*, 49). Jewel laughs at Donally's comment, but the question remains as to why, given this warning, he would consent, at Donally's request, to rape Marianne as a method of incorporating her into the Barbarian community.

Robert Clark accuses Carter of chauvinism in subjecting her female characters to moments of male domination such as this and warns that Marianne's response, pretending she does not exist, "effectively means that the victim can offer neither physical nor moral resistance."[10] Clark adds that when rape is "tinged with eroticism it represents subjection as part of desire and in itself desirable."[11] Although this may be an underlying motif in "bodice rippers," Carter is certainly not making an erotic spectacle of the scene, nor is she denying Marianne the voice of resistance. Marianne feels humiliated and violated, as Jewel and Donally indeed have intended. The attack on her is savage, made more so by Marianne's thoughts of both her snakebite and her brother's death. The rape is meant by Donally to "establish a common ground" in order that she and Jewel can "communicate as equals" (HV, 54), although the absurd niceties of the sentiment hardly fool Marianne, whose response to the rape is vitriolic. Totally without the natural compassion of Rousseau's noble savage, Jewel perpetrates this barbaric action. The horror of the situation is made quite clear: despite her strength of character, Marianne can be physically victimized, although as a method of gaining power over her spirit, the rape is a failure.

All of the imagery surrounding Marianne is traditionally masculine, as all of the imagery surrounding Jewel is traditionally feminine. The rape, however, is clearly a male act perpetrated on a female body and is a violent display of power causing a good deal of blood. Jewel calls it a "necessary wound" (HV, 55), one that connects Marianne to the demonic scene of dismemberment in the kitchen. Given that she is portrayed as having male attributes, her bleeding wound may indicate that she has been symbolically castrated. Freud suggests that little boys who catch sight of female genitals may well see in them a threat to their own.[12] For Jewel, Marianne certainly becomes a literal femme fatale, a woman who will cause his death, and he is clearly both attracted to and repelled by her. But here, even before he recognizes her as the girl who watched him kill her brother, Jewel admits that he has raped her because he is frightened of her. The rape is a way of reducing his fear and proving his heroism. But Donally has incited the act as one of incorporation, clearly a female image, as opposed to the male one of penetration, and given Donally's insistence that she is a *vagina dentata*, Jewel seems to be exhibiting the sort of female masochism so common to women in the Bristol Trilogy. And Jewel and Donally clearly come close to a prophetic truth. Marianne does, in a figurative sense, castrate Jewel, and although he does not know it in this particular scene, she will take his power, and Donally's, and she will end up both pregnant with Jewel's child and wielding the powerful "rod of iron" (HV, 150) over the entire tribe.

Marianne's subsequent erotic attachment to Jewel is perhaps more of a logical problem, especially given her response to Mrs. Green's request that Marianne be kind to him: "yesterday he jumped on me with appalling brutality, he has the hands of a butcher and eyes like trick mirrors" (*HV*, 70). The couple exchanges mutual declarations of hate, but once Marianne sees that Jewel thinks of her as an angel of death, she gains ascendancy. Their sexual couplings are described in terms of extinction and annihilation, but it is interesting that Marianne's discovery of her extraordinary powers happens only when "the dark removed the dangerous evidence of Jewel's face" (*HV*, 87). In her perceptions of it, Jewel's face is both protean and incomprehensible. She cannot read anything behind his eyes, and when she touches his face, she has no sense that it is real. Apart from the satisfaction of her desire, which is itself sometimes "an instrument solely of vengefulness" (*HV*, 89), Marianne protects herself by denying Jewel an existence outside their sexual coupling. As he leaves on his ill-fated rescue attempt, she is satisfied that she has destroyed him. In the light of reason, of which she is reminded by the lighthouse she sees on a cliff overlooking the sea, Jewel's "defiant construction of textures and colours" (*HV*, 147) dissolves. Marianne's attraction to Jewel was based on his exoticism, but once he is too tired and sick to maintain the mask of a perfect savage, she ceases to have any respect for him. Her revenge is complete.

The Rod of Iron

Despite the rape and the attempted rape as signs of machismo, Marianne never submits to fear. Perhaps as a way of dealing with a strange place and strange people, Marianne accepts Mrs. Green's description of the Barbarians as children. Marianne weeps at the death of a baby and even at the moment she realizes that Jewel has gone to certain death; but she keeps herself largely at an emotional distance. She is like Donally, whose position she will usurp, but she will not rely on charms, amulets, or the appearance of magic to maintain control. Her pregnancy—that she is producing Jewel's child—will give her the power to rule the Barbarians.

The Barbarians obviously see some aspects of femininity as alarming because they adopt the female costume of painted faces and plaited hair on their raids to make them more frightening. Apart from Mrs. Green, who was not born into the community, the Barbarian women seem to have no role in running it. Even Mrs. Green is powerless to intervene in the intended rape although she tries to do so. The women bear children, embroider cloth, prepare animal skins for clothing, and wait for their men to return from raids. Women also die in childbirth and occasionally produce deformed babies who are abandoned in the woods. Professor women are objects of fear in Barbarian lore, which asserts that Professor women not only harbor toothed vaginas but also do not bleed if cut. Marianne survives the bite of a viper, and this affront to nature makes her especially frightening to the Barbarians, who make a sign against the evil eye whenever she approaches. Jewel explains to Donally that when she watched Jewel kill her brother, her very act of looking at Jewel transformed him. Marianne, then, is not only Eve but also Medusa, who, as Barbara Creed points out, is regarded as "a particularly nasty version of the vagina dentata": "the Medusa's entire visage is alive with images of toothed vaginas, poised and waiting to strike."[13] Both sexually and symbolically, Marianne is a threat. In this context, the rape is an inverse revenge. Far from gaining power over Marianne, Jewel loses his power in the act.

Because the women are most intimately associated with various kinds of horror, it is not surprising that the men would take on the appearance of parodic women in order to terrify their enemies. But even without his makeup, Marianne calls Jewel a "phallic and diabolical version of female beauties of former periods" (*HV*, 137). If he is a "phallic" woman, however, his female masquerade is a nasty insult, designed to point out the power that, for the Barbarians, biological women lack.

It is significant that Marianne makes this statement as she and Jewel walk on the beach between two prewar relics. One is a ruined statue of a female beauty of a former period, a huge representation of a buxom woman in a bathing suit holding in her arms a stopped clock. The other is a lighthouse whose light is extinguished but is nonetheless "intransigent" (*HV*, 139), in which Marianne finds a potent symbol of her resolve to "go in fear of unreason" (*HV*, 139). To reject the statue as a symbol is to reject the kind of objectification the statue represents. Jewel may be "doomed to be nothing but an exhibit" (*HV*, 124), but Marianne refuses to be put upon as the focus for superstition, as a victim of violence, or as a dependent. No judgment is made as to the state of the community under Marianne's rule. The world is accelerating toward an entropic ruin that will not be altered by Marianne, but she might create the kind of complex system, a mixture of Professorial logic and Barbarian exoticism, that might allow a temporary respite from chaos.

Chapter Five
The Sweet Smell of Excess:
The Infernal Desire Machines of Doctor Hoffman

The Infernal Desire Machines of Doctor Hoffman (1972) is perhaps the most intellectually challenging and the most densely woven of all Carter's novels. It is a science-fiction fantasy that draws on the elements of satire as well as on the picaresque and Gothic genres. The characters seem to leap fully formed from the nightmare visions of Hieronymous Bosch, and the novel invokes intertextual references to, among others, Freud, Sade, *Gulliver's Travels*, Jorge Luis Borges, and Claude Lévi-Strauss, and to numerous composers, including Bach, Mozart, Beethoven, Berlioz, and Wagner. The novel has an engaging plot that moves from one absurdity to another, an abundance of eroticism, a good deal of violence, a quirky sense of humor, and an explosive ending. It is, in short, exhausting.

The Infernal Desire Machines expands upon the conflict between reason and unreason that appears in *Heroes and Villains*. In a letter quoted by Lorna Sage, Carter describes the book's "dialectic between reason and passion, which it resolves in favour of reason,"[1] although it is important to note that this opposition is not an evaluative one. Neither reason nor passion is good or evil; each has its complexities, its moments of boredom, and its dangers. It is also the case that neither is entirely discrete. The first chapter sets up the conflict between Doctor Hoffman and the Minister of Determination. The Doctor is intent on liberating desire; the Minister, on regulating empirical reality. As an allegorical conflict, this could be characterized in a number of ways as a dispute between the pleasure principle and the reality principle, idealism and empiricism, Dionysus and Apollo, anti-Enlightenment and Enlightenment, and any number of other binary oppositions. Trying to pin down the exact parameters of the opposition is, the novel suggests, essentially fruitless. The Doctor comments that his world (and, one might add, the fictional world he inhabits) is composed not of either/or, but of "and + and."[2] The Doctor and the Minister are themselves examples that these binaries are not fixed. Despite being the "most rational man in the world" (*IDM*, 24), the Minister has "all the Faustian desires" (*IDM*, 28), presumably for moments of delight. Similarly, Doctor Hoffman, whose task would seem to require a fecund and capricious imagination, is a dull, gray totalitarian. As Brian McHale puts it, "what had been posed as a polar opposition proves to be a complex and paradoxical interpenetration."[3] Setting up this polar opposition only to demolish it is one of the postmodern techniques Carter employs, and its purpose is to engage the reader's self-consciousness about what she or he does when confronted with such oppositions. The novel is indeed an allegory, but one of reading, of desiring, and of desiring through reading.

Plot and Narrative

Desiderio calls his tale a picaresque adventure, and it certainly recalls another famous example of the genre, *Gulliver's Travels*, both textually and structurally. The story is told episodically as Desiderio moves from one strange world to another. Unlike Gulliver, whose approval of the communities he visits is sometimes sycophantic, Desiderio enters into different societies while maintaining a sense of skepticism, and this is often all he has to keep himself out of danger. The novel opens with Desiderio's introduction of himself as the narrator. A national hero for his role in ending the Reality War, he is now an old man writing his memoirs in preparation for death. In his younger days, he was an assistant to the Minister of Determination in an unnamed South American city whose affluence and security were threatened by Doctor Hoffman's attack on reality. Young Desiderio's part in ending this attack is the substance of Old Desiderio's memoirs. Looking back on this story with weariness and the accumulated misery of a lifetime, Old Desiderio infuses his tale with cynicism. This is also a narrative of lost love, and Desiderio recounts the circumstances leading up to and away from his beloved Albertina in minute detail. Although he questions his failing memory, the detail underlines the obsessive nature of his love and the sweet self-torture it is to remember her.

Doctor Hoffman creates phantoms that are the concretization of the entire city's unconscious fantasies, and soon no one is able to tell the difference between reality and simulation. Watches become flowers, people see dead relatives walking down the street, sugar tastes like salt, and nothing is as it seems. In fact, the Reality War is a war against empiricism, because none of the senses can be relied upon. After three years, the city has deteriorated into a state of dissipation precisely because the senses are so unreliable that life cannot continue as it has done. There is no method of distinguishing reality from the projection of one's own or others' fantasy lives, although the Minister tries to treat the problem scientifically. Anything that enters his laboratory and dies as a result of his tests must have been real. Calling to mind the techniques used in Salem witch trials, the Minister's labs prove reality by killing it. In desperation, the Minister and Desiderio meet with the Doctor's ambassador, who promises an escalation of the siege. As a last resort, the Minister sends Desiderio on a top-secret mission, complete with forged papers and identity, to assassinate Doctor Hoffman.

Desiderio's first stop is a small town in which his cover is that he has been sent to investigate the mayor's disappearance. Here he meets the peep show proprietor, who was once Doctor Hoffman's professor but is now old and blind and the curator of a peculiar museum. The images in the peep show are Doctor Hoffman's samples of psychic possibilities, and they involve surreal scenes of sexuality, death, and cruelty. Desiderio spends the night in the mayor's house being seduced by the mayor's somnambulist daughter, Mary Anne. The next day, her body is discovered washed up on the shore, and Desiderio is charged with her murder, not just because he is discovered with the body, but because his captors have discovered he is not who he says he is. This latter is almost as suspicious a crime as murder, although Desiderio is not the murderer. Escaping his captors, he finds himself among the River People, who take him in, tend to his injuries, and treat him as one of their own. Only when he discovers that they intend to kill and eat him does he escape and meet once more with the curator of the peep show. Together, Desiderio and the curator travel with a carnival, and although Desiderio finds affection among some of his companions, he is savagely raped by the Acrobats of Desire, and afterward he stumbles to a cliff and takes refuge in a small cave. While he is recovering, a landslide obliterates the town, the carnival, and the peep show, and Desiderio emerges from his cave to find himself alone.

His next encounter is with the Erotic Traveller, a count whose sexual and other appetites recall both Dracula and the Marquis de Sade. The Count is an extraordinary narcissist, excessive in all of his desires because he feels that his are the only ones that matter. The Count's valet, LaFleur, is syphilitic, as though his body has taken on the consequences of all the Count's lusts. Although the samples in the peep show have been buried, the Count seems to enact all of their savage sexual imagery. Nowhere is this exemplified more clearly than in the horrific brothel, where the women are "sinister, abominable, inverted mutations" (*IDM*, 132).

In this nightmarish setting, Desiderio finally meets Albertina, Doctor Hoffman's daughter. Although Desiderio has already met her in dreams and in innumerable disguises, she appears to him in the brothel as the object of all his passions. The moment of recognition is short-lived, however, because the Determination Police are still hunting for Mary Anne's murderer and have traced Desiderio to the brothel. He flees with the Count and LaFleur to the coast, where all three board a ship. Attacked by pirates whose celebratory drinking bout leaves the ship to founder and sink, the travelers are washed up on the shore of Africa, where a band of cannibals boils the Count for soup. As they drag LaFleur to the same fate, however, Desiderio sees that he is Albertina in disguise, and stabs LaFleur's captors, embraces Albertina, and shoots the cannibal king. There is, in this scene, the sort of macho excess one finds in the films of Erroll Flynn. *The Infernal Desire Machines* is not a funny book; the persistent presence of sexual degradation and mutilation disqualifies it as a comedy. Moments such as this, however, seem taken straight out of the most clichéd B-movie in tone if not in substance, and one cannot help but laugh at their very excessiveness. Carter combines comedy and tragedy in what might be considered the most inappropriate of places. When Shakespeare gives the porter a comic turn in *Macbeth,* or when comic moments enter into other tragedies, the comedy provides relief from scenes of destruction, death, usurpation, and general discord. The comic moment may turn the audience's attention away, however briefly, from such scenes. Carter does not structurally separate comedy and tragedy, and this is one of the reasons critics have looked askance at her work. In the midst of really dreadful moments or even merely serious ones, she will pun or use inversion or draw the reader's attention to excess with a kind of gallows smile. This technique is not slapstick, and it does not make the reader's attention waver from the concerns at hand; as opposed to Shakespeare, Carter's comedy and tragedy happen in the same breath, in the same scene, and are responses to the same moment. The laughter may be surprising, and it may be uncomfortable, but my suspicion is that Carter was trying to create just such a response, a more sophisticated exploration, perhaps, of the laughter that accompanies a slip on a banana peel.

The penultimate chapter of *The Infernal Desire Machines* parodically invokes book four of *Gulliver's Travels,* in which Gulliver meets the rational—and by him much revered—Houyhnhnms. The creatures in Carter's novel are centaurs rather than horses, and they follow a strict adherence to the religion of the Sacred Stallion. They are rigorous Puritans who have a strong masochistic streak and pray that they will be reborn as horses rather than being imperfect combinations of horse and human. Never having seen humans, the centaurs do not know how to respond to Desiderio and Albertina but eventually decide to tattoo them with the likeness of the Sacred Stallion, nail iron shoes to their feet, and release them to their sacred herd of wild horses. Just as the centaurs are about to enact this ritual of hospitality, however, a helicopter appears and whisks Desiderio and Albertina to the Doctor's castle.

History and Fiction

The Infernal Desire Machines begins by drawing attention to the act of writing. Although Desiderio's story has been enshrined, he says, in the history books, he makes it clear that his retelling of his story will be different from the official accounts. History has constructed him as a hero and has tied up the loose ends of his adventures, but Desiderio's memoirs will presumably tell the story that official history cannot. Each is, in its own way, a partial, and therefore fictional, account. Nor will this story, narrated as it is by the story's subject, be a more realistic account, because Desiderio acknowledges that he is "no longer the 'I' of [his] own story" (*IDM*, 14). This story, then, will be historio*graphic* because it is a *written* history, and *meta*fictional because it draws attention to the parts of fiction and history that intertwine in a complex fabric. The reading and writing of both history and fiction come into play, and the reader is in this way invited to participate in the tale. A good deal of the novel is concerned with gaps (between event and memory, between desire and fulfillment and between history and fiction) as places where interpretive energy can flourish. The reader is encouraged to cross the gaps between fiction and history, language and desire, and the various selves of both the narrating and the experiencing Desiderio, although the novel's opening certainly informs the reader of the problems involved in such an enterprise.

The frame tale that opens and closes *The Infernal Desire Machines* appears to mediate between the reader's "reality" and the fiction to come. The frame tale presents the novel as an autobiography whose narrator appears, unmediated, as a guide to his life story. This is an illusion. Desiderio draws the reader's attention to fiction-making by undermining his confident assertion that he remembers everything perfectly. His past life, he says, is so complex that "it can hardly be expressed in language" (IDM, 11), and thus he immediately makes a distinction between what he remembers and what he will be able to communicate. What is to come will be both partial and biased, despite Desiderio's claim that he was once immune to any representation that was not empirically true. As he points out, his recollected self will be different from his narrating self.

At the beginning of the first chapter, Desiderio admits that he cannot remember exactly how the Reality War began, and by the time of the penultimate chapter, his narrative almost sounds like a fairy tale: "There was once a young man. . . ." (IDM, 166). The gaps in his perfect remembrance are made even clearer in his discussion of Albertina. The focus of his story and of his insatiable desires, Albertina is nonetheless a woman that "only memory and imagination could devise" (IDM, 13). His desire for her is consuming yet impotent and is the background against which his autobiography will be narrated. Because in his world all objects are emanations of this desire, the following narrative will hardly be a realist one. Because desire itself is inarticulable, Desiderio is pointing to his narrative as constructed by an imperfect memory, and by a narrative voice rendered inarticulate by the complexity of his desire. Given just how articulate Desiderio is about his adventures, and how detailed his reminiscences are, the area of desire is one that even he cannot put satisfactorily into words. He has no trouble describing cruelty, disaster, or miseries of various kinds, but desire eludes his descriptive powers, and that he is so detailed about most of his adventures underlines that nothing in his store of language can adequately capture what it is to desire.

Desire

Textual Desire

The intended result of Doctor Hoffman's machinations is to liberate the unconscious so as to liberate humankind. His project would seem laudable: all one's desires would be fulfilled, and all one's wishes would come true. One might imagine that the man who can turn theater audiences into peacocks and send painted horses from their frames to graze in the town square must be a magician indeed. To have one's dreams come true would seem to be purest joy, yet when Desiderio arrives at the Doctor's castle, he feels only profound disillusionment. Not only is the Doctor dull and gray in both appearance and personality, but when Desiderio first sees the Doctor, he is holding the hand of his embalmed wife, whose corpse he keeps on a settee. Desiderio realizes that he is in the presence "of the disciplined power of the utterly irrational" (*IDM*, 199). Like Dorothy in *The Wizard of Oz*, Desiderio feels that he has arrived at the "power-house of the marvellous, where all its clanking, dull stage machinery [is] kept" (*IDM*, 201). Far from being a liberator, the Doctor is a totalitarian who keeps scores of lovers in perpetual erotic motion, collecting the secretions that fall through the mesh of their cages to fuel his generators. One of these cages is to be Desiderio's marriage bed: in the Doctor's unique energy field, the consummation of Desiderio's love for Albertina will provide enough explosive fuel to complete the Doctor's plans. Desiderio kills them both.

The Reality War disconnects words from their meanings and celebrates the gap between them. The Minister fights back by trying to make everything identical with its name. Because desire, unlike need or want, cannot be named, the Minister hopes to eliminate desire by making empiricism the rule of order. The Reality War presents an interesting conundrum for the reader of a fiction whose words are intended to invoke multiple meanings. Language itself is indeterminate, as Ferdinand de Saussure theorized; it is a social contract. In the *Course in General Linguistics*, Saussure argues that the relationship between the word in its graphic or spoken form (the "signifier") and the thing the word represents (the "signified") is purely arbitrary.[4] For example, English speakers agree that a barking, four-footed animal is a dog, whereas other languages use other words for the same concept. In fiction, words symbolize things, but were words really identical to those things, interpretation would be a simple and unitary matter. At the gap between word and thing, between signifier and signified, the reader interacts with the text; the consummation of the two produces interpretive energy. From a postmodern perspective, the gap and its multiplicity are to be celebrated.

Because, given the evidence of her fiction, it is highly unlikely that Carter would agree with the Minister, one wonders why the effects of liberating desire are so dire. Once the city is in the grip of unconscious fantasy come to life, the city is almost on the verge of death. Cholera and typhoid ravage the populace, as do confusion and paranoia. If much of Desiderio's adventure is a projection of his own desires, then some of his desires are ugly—incest, rape, murder, cannibalism, and sadism; in each chapter, a death is imminent or actual. Albertina tells Desiderio that her disguises have been maintained by the force of his desire, and although she is the woman he loves, the force of his desire, if such it be, causes her rape by the Count and later puts her at the mercy of the centaurs. When unleashed, then, desire can be monstrous. So here there would appear to be a contradiction: desire in reading is to be courted; desire in "life" to be avoided. The difference, however, is that one might read in order to feel desire, in order that some interpretations will lead to fulfillment but in the recognition that there are others still to come.

Although he does not use the same methods as the Minister, Doctor Hoffman also strips the psyche of desire, but he does so by presenting its actuality. Actualized desire is chaotic. One might imagine, however, that with all one's wishes fulfilled by the Doctor's rubric, the ultimate result would be a kind of historical stasis. As Albertina says when she and Desiderio see pictures of Trotsky composing the *Eroica* Symphony and Van Gogh writing *Wuthering Heights*, "these are some of the things that everyone will perceive to *have always been true*" (*IDM*, 198, emphasis added). Like the Minister's empiricism, the Doctor's liberation will eventually fix meaning in a static system. The difference, for Desiderio, is that the Doctor has allowed the unconscious free play, whereas the Minister denies the unconscious outright. Desiderio's killing Doctor Hoffman is the Minister's triumph. Time begins again, and the city continues on in a state of gentle contentment that might also be called boredom. The citizens "do not know how to name their desires, so the desires do not exist" (*IDM*, 207). For Desiderio, however, who has been given the chance to name his desire, the disillusionment is profound. In essence, he has killed Albertina so that he may be able to continue to desire, despite the impotence and desperation that desire produces.

Beyond the Pleasure Principle

In "The Acrobats of Desire," Desiderio, disguised as the nephew of the peep show proprietor, joins a traveling carnival. The peep show is put together from a sack of samples that seem to prefigure events, although Desiderio is not sure whether they reflect or create his desires. In his explorations of the sack, he concludes that the samples represent all that it is possible to believe "by the means of either direct simulation or a symbolism derived from Freud" (*IDM*, 108), and the novel certainly depends on the complexities of psychoanalytic theory for much of its symbolism. One cannot, of course, wander too far into the permutations of unconscious desire without encountering Freud, and whereas the psychoanalysis of a fictional character is fraught with difficulty, Carter does provide enough information to tease the reader in such a direction. Psychoanalytic theories are perhaps put to better use in trying to explain the dynamics of the novel itself, its structure, and the place of the reader's desire. Carter replicates psychological processes in her novel, so that the reader is to Desiderio as Desiderio is to Doctor Hoffman.

One of Doctor Hoffman's particular triumphs is his play with time. The unconscious is the repository of things past, and yet it follows no formal temporal structure. Doctor Hoffman seeks to replicate this in "nebulous time," where all past events become present. Reading, however, which is the way we apprehend all of this, is an inescapably sequential event; as a picaresque hero, Desiderio moves forward through time in the novel. Here, then, are two impossibilities. Desire is inexpressible because as soon as it is articulated, it ceases to be desire. Time is so malleable that it can become nebulous, and yet Desiderio—and the reader—move very clearly through time to the end of the novel. If both nebulous time and desire are unrepresentable, how does one represent them in language?

Desiderio prides himself both on his immunity to the Doctor's images and on his memory. Neither of these, however, is shown to be particularly reliable. That Desiderio has an active unconscious store of images is obvious, and though his memory may be suspect, his unconscious uncannily repeats precisely the same situation over and over. Although his journey moves forward, his search is for his origins. In each chapter, the narrative repeats the structure of birth, entry into a community dominated by a male figure, and then a narrow escape from death. This specific structure calls to mind Freud's essay "Beyond the Pleasure Principle" (1920), in which he argues that mental processes are regulated by the pleasure principle. Given this, Freud wonders why painful experiences, repressed in the unconscious, should manifest themselves through repetition in dreams and behaviors. Although in children this can be an attempt at mastery, Freud speculates that in adult life the instinct to repeat is an "expression of the conservative nature of living substance."[5] Moreover, he suggests, *an instinct is an urge inherent in organic life to restore an earlier state of things.*[6] What lies beyond the pleasure principle, ultimately, is the death instinct, the ultimate drive toward the earliest, inorganic, state of things. Peter Brooks uses Freud's hypotheses to construct a model of narrative desire. Brooks suggests that "what a reader engages when he responds to plot. . . . [is] an inter-action with a system of energy which the reader activates."[7] The place of desire in this model is twofold, because it is not only a desire to return to an earlier state of affairs but also a desire for death.

Desiderio's plot mirrors both of these desires. He begins his narrative in the presence of a death that will come "in a few months" (IDM, 13) and ends his tale by calling his memoirs a "fat book to coffin Young Desiderio" (IDM, 221). The plot moves forward in one sense but is often halted by repetitive detours and backward glances. Brooks makes the point that repetitions delay a narrative's forward motion, that they delay pleasure "to ensure that the ultimate pleasurable discharge will be more complete."[8] This would seem also to be the Doctor's strategy. Desiderio is frustrated in his attempts to consummate his love for Albertina, because the delay will lead to the explosion of eroto-energy that is to fuel the Doctor's final triumph. Although killing Albertina, of course, means that the consummation will never happen, the buildup to the killing gives some sense of the power of Desiderio's desire, one that is partially discharged in his narration.

The final set of repetitions comes from Desiderio's obvious desire for a return to his origins, which is most lyrically expressed in his sojourn with the River People. His own racial origin is one of the reasons for his characteristic disaffection; he is "of Indian extraction" in a city where the word " 'indigenous' was unmentionable" (IDM, 16). His mother was a prostitute and his father unknown. Because the white nuns who looked after him as a child vouched for him, his colleagues ignore his difference, but only among the River People does he fit in. That the nuns can say Desiderio is something other than what he is, and that everyone then conspires to believe what they say despite the evidence of their eyes, is a milder version of Doctor Hoffman's games with reality. In both cases, seeing is believing, despite the contradiction between the two. Desiderio joins the company of the River People, having escaped from imprison-ment through a chimney from which he emerges like a "baby suddenly popped from the womb" (IDM, 64). Injured and delirious, he is rescued by Nao-Kurai, a river dweller whose face resembles Desiderio's own. Before he slides into unconsciousness, he hears a woman's voice singing in a language that takes him back to his childhood.

The chapter begins with a long history of his country's colonization and its disastrous effect on the indigenous peoples. Desiderio's desires in this instance match those of a larger populace, which, like him, has been denied its identity. Sharing these desires, as well as the physical traits of the indigenous people, gives Desiderio a sense of belonging to a family. Both historically and personally, he seems to have found a home. Nao-Kurai's mother invites Desiderio to call her Mama, and the family welcomes Desiderio as a future son-in-law when he acknowledges an affection for nine-year-old Aoi. Desiderio's own mother had found his race an embarrassment, but here his race is the cause of his salvation. After their engagement, Aoi comes to his room at night to play teasing, erotic games, but Desiderio is soon sexually involved with Mama, a situation he describes as effecting his reconciliation with mothers. This symbolic Oedipal scenario stops short of killing the father figure represented by Nao-Kurai, but recognizes the threat that he poses; Desiderio discovers that the River People intend to make him the main course of his own wedding feast because they hope to incorporate into themselves his superior education along with his flesh. Once he realizes this, Desiderio slips into the amniotic water to be reborn again on shore.

A number of the images from this peculiar family romance appear in later sections of the novel. Mama and the other women paint their faces to look like stylized dolls. This, combined with their stiff and formal movements, prompts Desiderio to describe them as looking not fully human, an impression he will also have of the women in the brothel. The threatened cannibalism will reappear when the Count is boiled up for soup. In a more complex permutation, it will also appear in the cannibal king's description of his female army, whose members earn their stripes by killing and eating their firstborn. The structure of the River People's language is also important. They have no equivalent for the verb "to be," which Desiderio thinks of as taking the kernel from "the Cartesian nut" (*IDM*, 71). That "I think, therefore I am,"[9] is the answer to Descartes's pondering identity and that Desiderio seems to take on different identities throughout the novel would seem to raise one of the novel's important thematic concerns. The River People's language's lack of complex temporal indicators comes up again in "nebulous time," which seems to favor a similarly "simple past and . . . continuous present" (*IDM*, 71). Finally, although Desiderio sleeps with his "Mama," without killing his father, the Oedipus myth is played out in Desiderio's killing Doctor Hoffman. All of these repetitions of imagery and structures have the effect of twining the reader's desire with Desiderio's. As the models of Freud and Brooks suggest, the reader experiences pleasure in moving *forward* to ascertain the novel's meanings while paradoxically realizing, as the peep show proprietor says, "the way South lies along the

Northern road" (*IDM*, 112). The interruptions, philosophical discourses, and repetitions retard pleasure only to increase it: "repetition can takes us both backward and forward because these terms have become reversible: the end is the time before the beginning."[10] In the novel's circular structure, invoked by the frame tale, the reader does indeed end the novel at the place of beginning, with Old Desiderio. Because he has purported to be writing his memoirs of a time before the narrative began, his last words proffer a place "before" the beginning, the reappearance of Albertina, who has been the ostensible driving force behind both his and the reader's desires.

Reading Female Desire

Albertina's desires are important because they are so problematic. In the land of the centaurs, she is raped by all the males in the village with such ferocity that she takes weeks to recover. She is convinced, however, that these beasts are "emanations of her own desires" (*IDM*, 186), and it is hard to read this without rushing to the conclusion that Carter is implying something utterly untenable. To do so would, I think, be to ignore the entire corpus of Carter's writing. One would be hard-pressed to accuse Carter of denigrating women or of being prudish about women's sexual desires. The evidence of *The Sadeian Woman* alone would mitigate against such accusations. Later in the novel, when Albertina tells Desiderio that her own disguises have been kept in place by *his* desires, there is a clue to solving the problem.

The description of the city in which the novel begins, combined with Desiderio's history of the indigenous population, introduces the theme of colonization, which, in its political sense, is not entirely played out. What is emphasized, however, is that Doctor Hoffman is a colonizer of the imagination; he attempts to confine the imagination and structure it according to his own samples. Whether the images of women in the novel are meant to be the emanations of Desiderio's or of the Doctor's desires is unclear, but what *is* clear is the male colonization of female desire. This is not to ignore women's construction of their own desires but to make the point that Albertina's desires may well have been drawn from a construction of women not of her own making. The samples in the peep show, the women in the brothel, the women warriors, and the female centaurs are all misogynist fantasies. Just as modern media create mass-produced constructions of women, Doctor Hoffman and Desiderio provide Albertina with the ready-made limits of her subjectivity, including the rape fantasy. More often than not, she is either a subordinate or a victim, and she is even denied her female body in having to be disguised as both a man and a hermaphrodite.

In *The Sadeian Woman*, Carter writes that "sexual relations between men and women always render explicit the nature of social relations" (*SW*, 20). What better place to explore and critique these relations than in a novel that makes clear the permutations of desire. Although *The Sadeian Woman* was published seven years after *The Infernal Desire Machines*, the ideas of the later book would seem to be anticipated in this novel. Given that desire here is gendered as male, Carter seems to be exploring the effect on women of releasing those desires. In this context, Doctor Hoffman takes on the cast of the pornographer who "reinforces the false universals of sexual archetypes": as pornography "reduces the actors in the sexual drama to instruments of pure function, so the pursuit of pleasure becomes in itself a metaphysical quest" (*SW*, 16). This could well be a description of Desiderio's quest for the consummation of his desire for Albertina, which can only be achieved if he accepts the Doctor's invitation to become himself a caged instrument of "pure function."

Disguise and Identity

When he is found with the body of Mary Anne and accused of her murder, Desiderio is also charged by the Determination Police with impersonating a government official. Under the Minister's rules, anything or anyone "seen to diverge significantly from it or his known identity is committing an offense" (*IDM*, 62). From the beginning of the novel, Desiderio so consistently diverges from his known identity that even it becomes only another in a long list of possibilities. One of the clues to the construction of identity in the novel is in Desiderio's comment that the language of the River People has no equivalent for the verb "to be." His reference to René Descartes in this context raises questions about just what it means "to be" and whether "I think, therefore I am" is an appropriate answer, given Desiderio's contention that he is not even the "I" of his own story. Shortly before he sees the caged lovers, Desiderio comes to understand the Doctor's version of Descartes's *cogito:* "I DESIRE THEREFORE I EXIST" (*IDM*, 211). Desire, however, is such a slippery concept that it hardly defines what it is "to be." In fact, various characters have their own versions of what defines being, and thus identity is shown to be amorphous.

In this context, even the most intimate of desires does not emanate from an essential kernel of self but is created by the interaction between self and world. One of postmodernism's most contentious areas of theoretical discussion has been in this area. Rather than the term "identity," postmodernist literary theory uses the term "subjectivity" to emphasize that the individual is subject to social and ideological forces over which he or she has little control. Among many other factors, one's biology, race, class, language, and education will all contribute to this self, which, rather than being essential, is liminal because it is always becoming. Carter's consuming interest in theater and various other kinds of performance gives us a clue to her postmodern characterization. Like Honeybuzzard in *Shadow Dance*, both Albertina and Desiderio take on a number of roles, and Albertina is the object of both the peep show samples and Desiderio's desires. She is thus subjected to the parts she plays. This area of postmodern study has been contentious, as Patricia Waugh argues, because it is not surprising to those who have been denied a full sense of identity by virtue of race, class, or gender that they are subjected to forces beyond their control: "Such Others may indeed, *already* have sensed the extent to which subjectivity is constructed through the institutional dispositions of relations of power, as well as those of fictional convention."[11] Desiderio's race and Albertina's gender make them marginal, although Desiderio, at least, is granted the power of his desires in constructing Albertina. Even Desiderio, however, has a fluid identity, exemplified not only by the previously mentioned instances but also by his various disguises. Among the River People, he seems to come closest to what he wants to be, but this self is constructed by nostalgia, as well as by the desperation of his flight from a false accusation. Later, he becomes the peep show owner's nephew and the Count's secretary. When Desiderio and Albertina are rescued from the centaurs, and Albertina is greeted as the Generalissimo, Desiderio wonders if he is to be the General's batman. Doctor Hoffman's plans for Desiderio, however, would lock him into something absolute. Although, in the end, he chooses a city where all is "absolutely predictable" (*IDM*, 221), his painful desires do at least allow him to imagine possibilities.

The "Moral" Pornographer

If the Doctor is the kind of pornographer described in *The Sadeian Woman*, then is *The Infernal Desire Machines* itself creating the same kind of "mythic abstractions" (*SW*, 6) Carter sees as the danger of pornography? The novel does present some horrifying scenes of sexual degradation, and because readerly desires are also being engaged by the novel, it could well be accused of promoting such desires. *The Infernal Desire Machines* certainly takes part in the paradox of feminist postmodernism as Linda Hutcheon describes it: "we have to feel the seduction in order to question it and then to theorize the site of that contradiction."[12] For Carter, this distancing would even be possible for pornography, were it to abandon its false universals for commentary on real relations: "the more pornographic writing acquires the techniques of real literature, of real art, the more deeply subversive it is likely to be" (*SW*, 19). The "moral pornographer," then, "might use pornography as a critique of current relations between the sexes" (*SW*, 19), and Carter would seem to be making such a critique in this novel. As has been discussed, Desiderio's desires and the Doctor's samples create "mythic abstractions" of the women in the novel. The intertextual references—in themselves, perhaps, a sack of samples—suggest that these attitudes have historical and literary precedents. *The Infernal Desire Machines* does involve both seduction and critique, and Carter uses literary, specifically metafictional, techniques to draw the reader's attention to the subversive nature of her "pornographic" scenes.

In "The Erotic Traveller," Desiderio meets the Count, a character modeled on the Marquis de Sade. As his description makes clear, the Count is very much a figure constructed by language. His every movement is a "riveting work of art" (*IDM*, 122), and although he "had scarcely an element of realism . . . he was quite real" (*IDM*, 123). He is narcissistic and misanthropic and describes himself as an artist whose material is flesh. He is, in short, the male principle taken to its absolute extreme; his sexual desires are exercises not so much in pleasure as in power. This is what Carter finds so interesting in Sade. Not only does he describe "sexual relations in the context of an unfree society as the expressions of pure tyranny" (*SW*, 24), but he encourages women "to fuck as actively as they are able, so that powered by their enormous and hitherto untapped sexual energy they will be able to fuck their way into history and, in doing so, change it" (*SW*, 27). To think of the Marquis de Sade as a protofeminist may seem odd, but Carter's interest in him stems from his interest in women's sexual reality as political reality. The Count's episodes are described in literary terms in order to break the frame that might surround any titillation; there is nothing erotic about the Count's adventures. Metafictional techniques are designed to draw the reader's attention to the construction of the text he or she is reading; the relationship between the Count and Desiderio could be considered as one of text and reader. The Count's narcissism, as Desiderio says, "demand[s] a constant witness" (*IDM*, 127). By making it clear that this is indeed a fiction, not a slice of life, metafictional elements diffuse any eroticism in this section. Carter suggests that Sade himself very rarely makes sexual activity seem attractive: he "has a curious ability to render every aspect of sexuality suspect, so that we see how the chaste kiss of the sentimental lover differs only in degree from the vampirish love-bite that draws blood" (*SW*, 24). It is interesting that the Count's horrifying encounters in the House of Anonymity are juxtaposed with Desiderio and Albertina's first kiss. Although the Count is very obviously an excessive character, his activities are not so different from those to which Desiderio subjects Albertina by the force of his desires because each involves objectifying women. The romanticism of this first kiss hardly compensates for the Count's sexual torture of a woman who is no more than a pulpy mass of meat. The women in the brothel are "as circumscribed as a figure in rhetoric" and have been reduced to an "ideational femaleness" (*IDM*, 132). Albertina is similarly "inexpressible" (*IDM*, 13) as a woman, and because she is the madam of the brothel, her first ecstatic encounter with Desiderio foreshadows disillusion.

Conclusion

When Desiderio sees the machinery behind the Doctor's apparent magic, Desiderio is so disappointed that even the promise of Albertina is not enough to lure him into a lovers' cage. Like the Doctor, Carter reveals the machinery behind desire, sexuality, and reading, and as a consequence, one might wonder whether her readers are in for a similar moment of disillusionment. In *The Sadeian Woman*, Carter suggests that the pornographer has the power to become a "terrorist of the imagination" (*SW*, 21) whose purpose would be to "reinstitute sexuality as a primary mode of being rather than a specialised area of vacation from being" (*SW*, 21–22). The Doctor is certainly a terrorist, although his aim is not to question reality but to institute a replacement for reality that will differ in content, perhaps, but not in form. Carter's own "terrorism" would celebrate disillusion if it was an ongoing process designed to combat the myths exemplified by the Doctor's samples. The illusions presented therein seek to mystify sexual relations; Carter's postmodernism seeks to reveal the mystification and its dangers. The novel courts disillusion as a necessary correlative to change.

Chapter Six
Out of Eden: *The Passion of New Eve*

Carter described *The Passion of New Eve* (1977) as "so ambitious, so serious and so helplessly flawed—flawed, I guess, partly because I started off writing the novel thinking I was interested in Myth with a capital M., . . . and ending up realising that Myth bored me stiff which is why Mother has a nervous breakdown when the revolution starts."[1] Like *The Infernal Desire Machines*, with which *The Passion of New Eve* reads as a companion piece, it is a serious intellectual critique of the symbols that "express the life within us."[2] Although the substance of that critique does not change in her next two novels, *The Passion of New Eve* is the last of Carter's works whose tone is so overtly didactic. Lorna Sage writes that Carter "sacrificed some of her habitual charm when she started to anatomize the androgynous zone she had so far contrived to inhabit."[3] Her subject is perhaps not one for which charm is appropriate; the novel is certainly breathtaking in its savagery. Carter's considerable intellect and literary skill are, in themselves, charms enough to weave an engrossing spell.

In *The Passion of New Eve*, Evelyn is indeed spellbound when he is transformed, against his will, into not only a woman but the object of his own desires. The novel is an overt attempt to reconsider the images and myths surrounding the construction of Woman, and it uses the genre of the picaresque novel to do so. The traditional picaro is, like Desiderio, a character who is an outsider and consequently in a position to comment as an outsider on the different societies in which he finds himself. The picaresque is a familiar genre in Carter's fiction, and she describes the genre as one in which "people have adventures in order to find themselves in places where they can discuss philosophical concepts without distractions."[4] This genre is usually narrated by a male character, although Carter turns this around in *The Passion of New Eve*: the male narrator finds himself transformed into a woman who is an outsider even to her- or himself. It is as if Desiderio were to wake up one day as Albertina. In such a case, he would be in a better position to understand the consequences of his fantasies. The genre is primarily a realist one whose object is satire, but Carter treats it to a postmodern perspective by complicating both realism and narrative voice. In fact, the novel questions the whole notion of the journey as progression from one place to another because neither beginnings nor endings are determinate.

Plot

Evelyn travels to America to take up a university teaching post in New York. The city he discovers is in a state of siege from within and is descending into chaos. Sewage systems are broken, huge rats roam the streets, and random, violent attacks are commonplace. Armed groups of newly created armies, one of which has occupied the university, battle one another. Evelyn befriends an old soldier, who practices alchemy and is beaten to death outside a supermarket. The night of his funeral, Evelyn follows Leilah, a black prostitute, the sight of whom has aroused him to savage desire, into the most ravaged part of the city. Their increasingly vicious erotic games are terminated by her pregnancy, which causes Evelyn to lose interest in her. An illegal abortion sends the bleeding Leilah into the hospital and eventual sterility, while Evelyn rushes to escape to the California desert on a quest for "that most elusive of chimeras, myself" (*NE*, 38).

When his car runs out of gas, Evelyn is captured and taken to Beulah, an underground city of Amazon women. Here, he meets Mother, Beulah's presiding deity, who rapes him in a ceremony that invites him to "Kill your father! Sleep with your Mother! Burst through all the interdictions" (*NE*, 64). Unlike Oedipus, however, Evelyn undergoes a castration that will turn out to be more than symbolic blindness. Mother is a surgeon who turns Evelyn into Eve through physical and psychological surgery. Mother plans to make Eve the new Virgin Mother by impregnating Eve with Evelyn's sperm. To this end, Mother seeks to help Evelyn into his womanhood through a program of rudimentary "psycho-surgery" (*NE*, 68). By watching Hollywood films, as well as by studying images of mothers and children, Eve is to learn what being both woman and mother means: Eve will be the new Virgin Mary, and will give birth to the "Messiah of the Antithesis" (*NE*, 67).

When the countdown to the moment of insemination is reaching its end, Eve makes her escape from Beulah, only to be captured again, this time by Zero and his harem. Zero is a madman who humiliates his wives and venerates his pigs. His first act upon capturing Eve is to rape her, thereby initiating her into his harem. Zero's seven wives love him because they believe that their weekly infusion of his semen keeps them healthy. They work hard to forage for food and supplies and even resort to prostitution to make enough money to support him. He forbids them from speaking, so they communicate in whispers and animal noises. Zero spends his days flying over the desert in a helicopter looking for the home of Tristessa St. Ange, the Hollywood star whom he blames for his sterility, whose death, he believes, will make him fertile. However, Tristessa was Evelyn's favorite movie icon, and Tristessa's films have been played to Eve in Beulah as part of her instruction in womanhood, so when Zero does find Tristessa, living in a glass house in the desert, Eve tries to protect her idol from Zero's rage. Eve cannot, however, protect Tristessa from Zero's derision, especially when he discovers Tristessa to be a man. The complexities multiply when in an impromptu ceremony, Eve, dressed as a man, is wedded to Tristessa, dressed as a woman, and afterward the two are forced to consummate their marriage. Together, they manage to escape in Zero's helicopter, and although Eve comes to think that Tristessa is quite mad, she loves him.

Lost in the desert, Eve and Tristessa suffer from want of water and fear of death. They next encounter a band of young soldiers who are fighting a religious war in the hope of restoring law and order to the "godless state of California" (*NE*, 157). Finding Eve and Tristessa locked in an embrace, the soldiers detain them for the crime of lechery. Tristessa, still a sexually ambiguous figure, reverts to his female self and kisses the colonel, for which transgression Tristessa is shot. Once more on the run, Eve finds herself in the middle of a civil war that has spread across the country from New York. Among the ruins of a shopping center, Eve is reunited with Leilah, now a member of a guerrilla army. Eve discovers that Leilah, renamed Lilith, is Mother's daughter. Mother has gone mad and lives on a beach, drinking vodka and singing. The last pages of the novel recount Eve's final rebirth. She is led by Lilith to a fissure in a rock and finds herself in a womblike labyrinth where time appears to go backwards. Emerging onto Mother's beach, Eve finds a plastic skiff and sets herself adrift on the ocean.

Narrative Structures

In the picaresque novel, the narrative is constructed as an autobiography, and the narrating voice is clearly attached to the character who is the protagonist of the story. In *The Infernal Desire Machines*, the certainty of the narrative voice is called into question because Desiderio is looking back on himself as a young man. The character about whom he writes is a very different self, Desiderio implies, from the character who is writing. *The Passion of New Eve* further complicates this issue because it is not clear whether the narrator is male or female; this is an important consideration, given Carter's interest in making reading a very active process. Guessing the gender of the narrative voice will reveal the reader's assumptions about language, perception, voice, and structure, and whether any of these elements can be said to reveal maleness or femaleness. Given that the narrator has been male and is female, it is not surprising that the narrative voice should be a site of conflict and confusion. Eve ponders the nature of the masculine and the feminine without any conclusion: "Though I have been both man and woman, still I do not know the answer to these questions" (*NE*, 149–50). In *The Sadeian Woman*, Carter quotes Emma Goldman, who writes that the demand for equal rights "will have to do away with the absurd notion of the dualism of the sexes, or that man and woman represent two antagonistic worlds" (*SW*, 151). Although such antagonism does not disappear from *The Passion of New Eve*, Goldman's notion of dualism is given a different perspective when male and female exist in the same body.

Eve narrates the story retrospectively, so her point of view would logically color those sections of the novel in which Evelyn is the prime actor. Because Eve begins life as Evelyn, the question remains as to whether the point of view of her narration has been from a male consciousness all along. This delightful confusion is Carter's most clever manner of making the reader consider what the signs of either a male or a female consciousness might be. Readers would have to decide whether there is a gendered use of language, of idiom, or of inflection, as well as think about whether the change in Evelyn's physical appearance would lead to a corresponding change in his manner of thinking.

There is a close relation between the complication surrounding the narrative voice and the structure of the narrative itself. Mother considers time to be male; she calls it a "phallic projectory" (*NE*, 53). This novel, to some extent, fulfills her dream of changing this aspect of time, but the chronology of the plot is even more complicated than Mother's ideal. The episodic structure of the novel breaks the illusion of progress and development on which realist narrative relies. Like *The Infernal Desire Machines*, this novel moves forward and backward, taking detours along the way. Although Eve's story ends where it began, with Mother, the mother Eve discovers is a very different woman from the one who ruled Beulah, and if Eve's intention in setting out on the ocean is to return to Evelyn's home, it will be a place where she has no history or identity as a woman.

The novel also critically revisits the history of Western literary representation. Intertextual references are drawn from the Bible, Greek and other mythologies, *Great Expectations*, *Wuthering Heights*, *Orlando*, and there are also references to Poe, Sade, Wagner, and Mahler, among others. The list provides a proliferation of voices and stories against which the transformation of Evelyn into Eve is effected. As Susan Suleiman points out, Carter "multiplies the possibilities of linear narrative and of 'story,' producing a dizzying accumulation that undermines the narrative logic by its very excessiveness."[5] The novel's intertextuality complicates linear narrative and linear time because readers have to read on many different levels at once. Mother's goal, to feminize time, involves a "journey backwards to the source" (*NE*, 53). Moreover, she assumes that this source is attainable as something stable, and as the novel makes clear, this assumption dooms her project to failure. Her own view of time is just as much unidirectional as the view of time she wishes to change.

Appearance and Essence

Just before his unwilling transformation into a biological woman, Evelyn asks, "does a change in the coloration of the rind alter the taste of a fruit?" (*NE*, 68). Despite the assurance of one of his captors that a change in his appearance will indeed alter his essence, the novel is much less certain. It explores the problems of appearance and essence, and examines the process by which Evelyn learns to adapt his (her) female body to his male history. As Evelyn becomes Eve, she (he) has to learn to be a woman because she is seen by others, and eventually sees herself, as a woman.

Beulah, the underground technological womb from which Eve is born, is a city of single-breasted women in the service of Mother, "the Castratrix of the Phallocentric Universe" (*NE*, 67). Her transformation of Evelyn into Eve suggests that appearance alone is not quite enough to produce essence. Evelyn has to be taught to be a woman, and his education consists of videotapes showing all possible paintings of the Virgin and Child as well as subliminal images designed to "instil the maternal instinct" (*NE*, 72). This education also involves telling stories about men's treatment of women's bodies: female circumcision, foot binding, suttee, "the horrors my old sex had perpetrated on my new one" (*NE*,

73), as Eve puts it. But most of all, and particularly because Eve's new body is formed by "concensus agreement on the physical nature of an ideal woman drawn up from a protracted study of the media" (*NE*, 78), the psycho-surgery is reinforced by showing Eve the movies of Tristessa St. Ange, "the most beautiful woman in the world" (*NE*, 5). Eve thus learns to be woman as cinema spectacle, framed, as it were, "by the look of the camera as icon, or object of the gaze: an image made to be looked at by the spectator, whose look is relayed by the look of the male character(s)."[6] In effect, Eve learns that she must accept being looked at as Evelyn once looked at women.

Persistence of Vision

Carter's use of cinematic imagery underlines the importance of looking and being looked at. One of the challenges facing film theorists, for instance, has been to consider the position of women who watch film and to theorize how female spectators can appropriate what has traditionally been considered the male gaze. *The Passion of New Eve* has much the same project. Because Eve has been trained to be a woman by watching Tristessa's films, Eve is clearly being instructed in a male vision of what a woman should be. Her response, therefore, is certainly going to be different from Evelyn's response to the same film. For Evelyn, Tristessa is erotic; for Eve, Tristessa is a lesson in the "shadowed half being of reflected light" (*NE*, 72). The powerful media images of women do indeed show the female spectator that she is an object to be looked at rather than the subject of an active gaze of her own. In *Alice Doesn't*, Teresa de Lauretis makes the point that "the project of feminist cinema . . . is not so much 'to make visible the invisible,' as the saying goes, or to destroy vision altogether, as to construct another (object of) vision and the conditions of visibility for a different social subject."[7] Such a project would articulate the position of the female spectator with regard to film and would raise the question of how to "reconstruct or organize vision from the 'impossible' space of female desire . . . and how to represent the terms of her double identification in the process of looking at her looking."[8] Given the importance of who *sees* and who *is seen* in the novel, consideration of the construction of looking is central to *The Passion of New Eve* and is a lens through which to examine how Eve/Evelyn sees and is seen. The multiple narrative possibilities cross paths with the imagery of sight and seeing in the thrice-repeated phrase "persistence of vision," which is always directly associated with Tristessa. The term comes from nineteenth-century attempts to explain why the eye perceives motion in film when there is, in fact, "nothing but a succession of still images."[9] The explanation at the time was that "a positive after-image from the first flash of a two-flash display is assumed to be still present when the second flash occurs. The continued existence of a positive after-image . . . makes possible the perception of continuous movement."[10] It was believed that the persistence of the retinal image would give the illusion of movement; whereas this theory is now considered an inadequate explanation of motion perception, it is interesting to consider the ideological implications that Carter seems to find in the term. As Lederman and Nicols suggest, "innumerable commentators have cited the impression of movement as a fundamental part of any cinematic appeal based on realism."[11] Here, though, persistence of vision is not realist. Like metaphor, persistence of vision carries over from one image onto another; Carter uses it to emphasize a *relation* rather than an inexorable forward movement. Indeed, the phrase is used in the novel to suggest a cinematic method of temporarily cheating time, of maintaining an appearance as essence. Film star Tristessa, for example, will always be beautiful as long as "celluloid remained in complicity with the phenomenon of persistence of vision; but that triumph would die of duration in the end, and the surfaces that preserved [her] appearance were already wearing away" (*NE*, 5).

But persistence of vision also acts on characters as well as on the reader. Rather like drawings that allow the viewer to see one of two images, but not both at once, persistence of vision encourages a back-and-forth reading. It puts earlier images in the context of later ones, and later images in terms of earlier ones. Such is the case with Evelyn's change of gender, particularly the moment at which Evelyn mis-recognizes his image. As a newly born woman, he looks for himself in the mirror but sees Eve, "a young woman who, though she was I, I could in no way acknowledge as myself" (*NE*, 74). This is Evelyn's first experience of gender as performance—a notion that has implications for narrative. On one level, Evelyn is the narrator and Eve the object of his desires. When Evelyn first sees Eve, he comments that Eve is a "*Playboy* center-fold" and his own "masturbatory fantasy" (*NE*, 75). Designating Eve as a *Playboy* centerfold seems clearly to indicate that the narrator here is male, and yet the various permutations of who is looking at whom are dizzying. To determine literally who sees and who speaks in this passage, one would have to enter into an unresolvable debate between mind and body. Here, as in many other parts of the novel, the

"I" who speaks or sees is indeterminate: "I" is simultaneously "not-I." Therefore, on another level, one could argue that as the retrospective narrator, Eve is narrating Evelyn's point of view on Eve. But in this case, the male gaze is outwitted because Eve looks back; as both narrator and character, she actively returns the gaze while looking at herself being looked at.

Women, Made or Born?

My interpretation of persistence of vision as a relation rather than as Mother's phallic projectory has implications for the construction of identity, which seems very much at issue here. Clearly Eve is not *born* but *made* a woman, and some of Evelyn's gestures and inflections remain until the moment when Eve learns to look at, touch, and explore herself as a woman. The identity, either of the narration or of the character, is formed in relation, as is the narrative itself, which comes to the reader, for example, already interpreted through the remarkably dense weaving of intertexts. The constantly shifting and often ambiguous multiple voices of the intertexts and the temporal indeterminacy of persistence of vision not only point out the multiplicity of narrative but also multiply the possibilities for gender beyond the absolutes of maleness and femaleness suggested by the one-eyed, one-legged, sterile Zero and the eight-breasted Mother.

The fluidity of gender is made most apparent and most ambiguous in the first five chapters, in which Evelyn's story is narrated through Eve's retrospective eye. When the British-born Evelyn lands in New York, he finds the city itself a narrative of discontent, "scribbled all over with graffiti in a hundred languages expressing a thousand different griefs and lusts and furies" (*NE*, 12). Evelyn is an innocent abroad in an apocalyptic landscape inhabited by gun-toting thugs and rats as "fat as piglets" (*NE*, 17). The city, he says, is a "metaphor for death" (*NE*, 15), and just as chaos and dissolution begin to reach unbearable limits, he meets Leilah. When Evelyn looks, especially at Leilah, his vision is to some extent determined by Eve's looking back on him looking at women. Because Eve is a woman when she tells Evelyn's story, her narration, of course, is tinged with the knowledge of what it is to be both the subject and the object of such a look.

The most interesting aspect of this first section of the novel is the complication of the narrative level. To some degree, the novel imitates the narrative structure of one of its intertexts, Charles Dickens's *Great*

Expectations, in that Eve is narrating in retrospect, yet she is both the *I* and the *not-I* narrator. Determining narrative level in the section of the novel that tells Evelyn's story depends entirely on whether the reader sees Eve as a man in a woman's body or as a woman, on whether a change in the coloration of the rind changes the essence or not. "Self," here, is an indeterminate concept of which neither Evelyn nor Eve is very sure. Indeed, the issue is further complicated because there are "feminine" qualities in Evelyn even before his metamorphosis, and "masculine" qualities in Eve after it. Evelyn describes himself as slender and delicate, and when Sophia dresses him in clothes like those worn by the women in Beulah, he says that he could have been her sister "except that I was far prettier than she" (*NE*, 55). Eve, who is "literally in two minds" (*NE*, 77) after her operation, comments "I would often make a gesture with my hands that was out of Eve's character or exclaim with a subtly male inflection" (*NE*, 101). And as Eve becomes "almost the thing [she] was" (*NE*, 107), she comments that even her memories are like the images from a movie seen a long time ago or clothes that no longer fit: "they were old clothes belonging to somebody else no longer living" (*NE*, 92).

There is no marked change of "voice" between the parts of the novel that concern Eve and Evelyn, although in both sections, comments are made about women's speech being incomprehensible. Leilah's speech is reported indirectly, and Evelyn says that he is unable to understand her: "her argot or patois was infinitely strange" to him (*NE*, 26). The women in Zero's harem are forced to utter animal noises because Zero believes that women are more primitive than men and closer to the animals, and so "our first words every morning were spoken in a language we ourselves could not understand" (*NE*, 97). And yet this too is reported speech that the reader does not actually read. The women must whisper to speak to one another, and because there is little female solidarity in the Church of Zero, even these whispers might be reported to Zero, who will beat the offender. Even the direct speech cannot easily be assigned to either male or female. The first sentence, for example, appears to be spoken by Evelyn: "The last night I spent in London, I took some girl or other to the movies and, through her mediation, I paid you a little tribute of spermatozoa, Tristessa" (*NE*, 5). Logically, the speaker must be Evelyn, because only Evelyn could pay such a tribute. Yet it could also be argued that the speaker is an Evelyn whose experiences are being remembered by Eve, whose distance from an "actual" Evelyn is made clear in the formality, almost parody, of the phrase "tribute of spermatozoa." At this point of retrospective telling, neither Tristessa nor Evelyn "exists" except in Eve's memory; each is re-created by Eve, who soon makes her presence known. The way in which she does so imitates Leilah's erotic journey through the labyrinthine New York streets.

As Evelyn, consumed with desire, follows her, Leilah leaves behind an Ariadne's thread of clothing dropped on the street for Evelyn to pick up: her dress, crotchless underwear, fur coat, and stockings. When Eve narrates the opening chapters, her narration itself becomes a kind of striptease when she drops clues about her voice and plot. She comments on Tristessa as an illusion, a fact that only Eve could know. She also makes references to hermaphrodites and complains that she was never schooled in the techniques of contraception when she was given a uterus of her own. These clues, Tiresias-like, prophesy something of the future, but they complicate the narrative. Like the discarded articles of clothing, Eve's snippets of information dropped along the way for the reader to pick up make it clear that the narrator is, and is not, Evelyn. While tempting the reader to pursue the erotic game, Eve's discarded clues do not lead the reader to a fulfillment of desire or to a specific answer to the question of just who is telling this story.

In almost every episode of the novel is a labyrinth, although this first, erotic journey to the heart of New York's darkest ruins is the first and most obvious. In Greek mythology, the labyrinth housed the Minotaur, a creature that was half man, half bull. Every nine years, seven young men and seven young women were given to the Minotaur as food. Theseus offered himself as one of the victims but was saved by Ariadne, who gave him a ball of thread that allowed him to find the Minotaur and, having killed him, to find his way out of the maze. When Evelyn follows Leilah into the most dangerous part of the city, he feels his fear as part of his desire for her, although he is, astonishingly, protected by an aura of innocence that seems to surround her. Evelyn's treatment of Leilah is brutal: he chains her and beats her, then ties her to the bed, leaving her feet free so she can kick away the rats. Sex between them leads to greater and greater yearning until, one day, Evelyn finds that he is bored. When he discovers Leilah's pregnancy, Evelyn cannot extricate himself from the relationship fast enough.

Each of the labyrinths seems to offer an answer to a question or a solution to a problem. At the heart of each labyrinth is something that seems to be a center or a culmination but is, like the Minotaur itself, a dual or even multiple being. Leilah has appeared to be the answer to Evelyn's desires, but when she is pregnant, and therefore not one but two, he flees. In the labyrinthine underground passages of Beulah, Evelyn finds another dualism in being given a double identity. At the center of Tristessa's house is also a dual being, Tristessa herself as both man and woman. Centers clearly fluctuate, and none of them provides a single solution. Eve's journey through a womblike labyrinth at the end of the novel seems to be a journey of self-discovery. The series of caves, some of which seem to be lined with flesh, is a place where time itself fluctuates. Eve narrates much of this section in the present tense, although what she finds in the caves is items from her past: a publicity photograph of Tristessa, a flask that reminds Eve of Evelyn's friend the alchemist, and the piece of alchemical gold that Evelyn bestowed on Leilah. In the last of a series of fleshy, pulsating caves, Eve seems to be observing time running backward. From this cave, she is expelled, crying for Mama, onto a beach where Leilah, who is now Lilith, awaits.

This final labyrinth is the most confusing of all, particularly because it seems to promise a revelation that it does not deliver. At the end of her journey, Eve finds Mother, who has now gone mad, sitting on the beach awaiting death. The interpretive conundrum surrounding the voice of the narrator is similarly labyrinthine. As in all of the mazes in the novel, the novel itself does not solve the problem but suggests that any solutions must themselves be multiple. Mother, who has sought singularity, has gone mad in the process, and time cannot go backward outside the peculiarity of the caves. When Eve leaves the shore in her little boat, she leaves Mother's mythology behind, possibly to create one of her own or, perhaps, to dispense with mythology altogether.

Gender as Performance

When, as a member of Zero's harem, Eve is subjected to Zero's violent coupling, she comments that she is forced to look back on what Evelyn once was and to know that Evelyn, too, was once a violator as Eve is now being violated. This suggests that she recognizes herself as both self and other. The novel does not suggest that there is any final reconciliation of these two; Eve is both and neither male and female. As I have argued, the fluidity of gender in the novel, in both the transsexual Eve and the transvestite Tristessa, accounts for some of the difficulties in determining narrative voice. Gender does not, in itself, determine narrative, but gender makes narrative identity as complex as gender itself. Both Eve and Tristessa learn to *perform* their genders, and the very act of performance suggests a liminality that would seem to argue against an

original essence. The wedding, in which Tristessa plays the bride and
Eve the groom, is the culmination of the performative images: "Under
the mask of maleness I wore another mask of femaleness but a mask
that now I never would be able to remove, no matter how hard I tried,
although I was a boy disguised as a girl and now disguised as a boy
again" (NE, 132). That this is also a description of the narrative in the
first five chapters of the novel further confounds attempts to determine
the narrative voice and implies that the narrative itself is a conscious
performance that reflects the shifting identities of the narrator(s).

In *Gender Trouble,* Judith Butler argues that gender "is the repeated
stylization of the body, a set of repeated acts within a highly rigid regu-
latory frame that congeal over time to produce the appearance of substance, of a natural sort of being."[12] Mother's fondest wish, to kill time
and live forever, is perhaps an effort to eliminate precisely those frames
that regulate gender. It is also clear that her project will fail, because
although Mother, like Eve, is a technological construction, she believes
in the essence of what her appearance conveys. For both Tristessa and
Eve, gender is a process of learning; for Mother, it is a static fact.

Nowhere is the stylization of the body made more apparent than in
the presentation of Tristessa, although both she/he and Eve sometimes
make the mistake of behaving almost too much like women. Zero, who
thinks of himself as the concrete fact of machismo, assumes that to be
too much like a woman is to show signs of lesbianism, which he hates to
the point of violence. When he first captures Eve, he examines her
closely because she seems almost too perfect to be real. Zero's sterility,
however, he blames on Tristessa, whose apparently female gaze has symbolically castrated him. In the movie theater where Zero watches
Tristessa perform the role of Emma Bovary, he thinks that her eyes have
consumed and doomed him. The "woman's" active gaze, as Zero sees it,
is not just a threat. When the woman looks back, she does so with
"toothed" eyes.

When Evelyn sees his new body, he sees it as the one he always
desired to possess as his other when he was a man. Evelyn's transformation is beyond his control, but Tristessa has performed Mother's psycho-
surgery on himself. He has constructed himself as the "shrine of his own
desires" (NE, 128). His ideal woman is a femme fatale, a combination of
beauty and suffering, "romantic dissolution, necrophilia incarnate" (NE,
7). The irony here is that the femme fatale has herself ambiguous conno-
tations, which Mary Ann Doane describes as "the fact that she never
really is what she appears to be."[13] Tristessa, despite his feminine man-

ners and appearance, is more fully androgynous than Eve. Eve does come to see herself as a woman through Tristessa's mediation, but Tristessa's gender remains a far more ambiguous performance. He parodies the feminine without becoming it. Lilith describes him as too much of a woman to undergo Mother's surgical transformation but notes, too, the paradox that only someone with an ineradicable sense of maleness could construct a woman such as Tristessa. Tristessa is the perfect woman, constructed out of purely male desires. He symbolizes a fabrication of gender that even he cannot put into narrative. When Tristessa narrates his own story, he distances himself from its subject, calling himself both "I" and "she," and creating for himself a fictional autobiography composed largely of his suffering. But even here there is no suture of identity; Tristessa's gender remains double. As Lilith muses to Eve, if Tristessa has indeed made Eve pregnant, the baby will be the child of two mothers and two fathers.

What is clear about both Tristessa and Eve, however, is the lack of an "original" gender. Butler argues that gender parody, as in transvestism, "is *of* the very notion of an original . . . so gender parody reveals that the original identity after which gender fashions itself is an imitation without an origin."[14] Zero and Mother are characters who, despite their self-construction as male and female incarnate, do see an essential identity. Each has eliminated, or wishes to eliminate, the "other." For Eve and Tristessa, though, gender cannot help being performative, because its liminality provides multiple possibilities.

Alchemy

Mother and Zero believe that perfection can be attained in the essence of either femininity or machismo. As such, they concur with the principles of alchemy introduced to the novel by the Czech soldier, Baroslav, who befriends Evelyn. Baroslav makes Evelyn a nugget of gold in an alchemical crucible that Evelyn later gives to Leilah, and the gold eventually buys the boat Eve uses to sail away. The gold is a reminder of the principle of flux and transmutation, but it is simultaneously a symbol of perfection.

Alchemical principles rely on Aristotle's theory of the four elements that constitute all matter: earth, air, fire, and water. These elements are in constant flux, alchemists believed, because everything in nature is always striving toward perfection. Gold was thought to be the most perfect of all the metals, so it was assumed that all other metals would try to attain a similar perfection. By manipulating the proportions of the elements that supposedly made up any metal, alchemy tried to speed up the inevitable progress to perfection by using the mediation of a mysterious substance called the philosopher's stone or the elixir of life. Alchemists believed that the world of matter functioned by means of opposing forces such as hot and cold, wet and dry, and male and female. Both Mother and Zero would appear to concur that these forces, especially male and female, are antagonistic. Zero's humiliation of his wives is based on his view that women are closer to animals than humans, and Mother's desire is to maintain the antithesis between male and female but to invert the hierarchy so that female is ascendant. The absolutism of these characters' division of the world recalls Doctor Hoffman, whose liberation is just another form of imprisonment. *The Passion of New Eve* celebrates flux rather than perfection. The uncertainty attending the narrative voice, the voices of the other novels, and even Evelyn's transformation into Eve all create a sense of chaos. Although this chaos has moments of order, it does not mean that the theme of the novel is a drive to perfection and hence to stasis. For Baroslav, the chaos exemplified by the dissolution of the city is simply a movement toward a new order. Evelyn sees Tristessa, whose movies he watches on television, as presiding over the entropy, whose end is death.

Tristessa and Eve, however, are both male and female and therefore seem to embody something beyond antithesis. Mother wants time to move backward toward the source, which, in her terms, is Mother Earth. Zero, too, seeks the source of his sterility, Tristessa, and wishes to murder her so that he may begin his repopulation of the world. When Eve and Tristessa flee to the desert, Eve calls them Tiresias, the figure from Greek mythology, who had also been a man and a woman and was able to prophesy the future. If Eve's child does indeed have two mothers and two fathers, the notion of origin certainly becomes complicated. Like the alchemists, Mother and Zero seek perfection, but while Eve must of necessity look back to her past as a man, she is simultaneously moving forward as a woman who is constantly becoming.

Stones in Glass Houses

When Zero and his harem descend on Tristessa's house, they find a shrine to misery. Surrounded by glass tears, the house contains a number of coffins housing waxwork figures of movie stars who have died from fame and other forms of violence. The house rotates, and the theme from *Gone with the Wind* is piped through the rooms. Tristessa is eventually discovered also lying in a coffin but only pretending to be dead. Emaciated and living on drugs and vitamins, he makes a spectacle of death and of suffering. As Eve remembers the tragic films in which she has seen him perform, it becomes clear that Tristessa does not differentiate between the roles he has played in the cinema and the role he plays outside it. As a woman, Tristessa is the grande dame of the tragic, martyred heroine, and his success as a film idol has been because he has played the woman who incarnates the "secret aspirations of man" (*NE*, 129). As such, Tristessa is the perfect woman because her solitary suffering produces a detached, erotic frisson.

In a glass house, everything would appear to be visible. Like the cinema, a glass house encourages and invites voyeurism. Tristessa, in fact, seems to thrive on the kind of gaze that caused Evelyn's erotic moment at the beginning of the novel. Despite being hidden in the desert, her glass house is a shrine to her visibility. Obviously, a film idol ceases to be a film idol if he or she is not seen, and Tristessa provides for the possibility of seeing and being seen even in an unpopulated desert landscape. When Zero arrives, Tristessa hides spectacularly, and once discovered, she takes on the inappropriate role of the gracious hostess to greet her visitors. Not knowing quite how to respond to this woman who has made herself a shrine to the male gaze, Zero and his harem desecrate the house and parody Tristessa's personae. The women dress in her gowns and cover their faces with makeup. These are only parodies, though, because as women, they are imperfect representations of themselves. Only Tristessa, a man, could construct the perfect woman. In this he is not unlike Eve, whose perfect body is also the reflection of a male ideal.

The question one might ask of the novel, then, is whether it is possible to be woman without being a male construct. The images of women the novel presents are no more attractive than are the images of men. Zero and Evelyn are sadistic and cruel, and the colonel of the children's religious crusade is almost a parody of militarism. Of the women, Mother is close to death at the end of the novel; she is blind and drunk and hardly the myth made flesh as she had originally presented herself. Her daughter, Lilith/Leilah, has become a soldier and is sterile as the result of her crude abortion. Eve and Tristessa make femininity a conscious effort, but they are the only "women" given significant space in the novel, and they are, after all, men. In the Bristol Trilogy, women are victims who take a masochistic enjoyment in their victimization; in *The Infernal Desire Machines*, *Heroes and Villains*, and this novel, women's position is shown, with some vitriol, to be a male fabrication. The narrative complexities are certainly part of feminist writing practice because they call into question the whole notion of how identity, male and female, is constructed. Even in Mother's ideal community, though, how to be a woman is still in the hands of media images. Although the critique of these images is a powerful one, it is not until *Nights at the Circus* that Carter explores the possibility of a woman who is in charge of her own image.

Chapter Seven

The Roar of the Greasepaint:
Nights at the Circus

Nights at the Circus (1984) is, for good reason, Carter's best-known and most acclaimed novel. It is witty and lush, and so exuberant in language and character that the novel gives the impression of bursting at its seams. None of the political or social concerns evidenced in Carter's previous novels have disappeared, but the tone of this novel is appreciably different from *The Passion of New Eve* and *The Infernal Desire Machines of Doctor Hoffman*. The writing here is consistently ebullient, and the story is completely engaging. Salman Rushdie suggests that in Carter's longer fiction, the "distinctive Carter voice, those smoky, opium eater's cadences interrupted by harsh or comic discords, that moonstone-and-rhinestone mix of opulence and flim-flam, can be exhausting."[1] However much one might agree with the objects of Carter's critique, the didacticism of some of her novels could be added to Rushdie's list as a source of exhaustion. *Nights at the Circus* could certainly be described using all of Rushdie's terms, but however complex, it is a novel whose end point is laughter rather than exhaustion. Like its aerialist heroine, the novel turns a good number of somersaults before its final bow.

The Plot as Aerialist

Much of the novel's raucous spirit is embodied in Fevvers, a winged aerialist whose feathered appendages give rise to her slogan, "Is she fact or is she fiction?"[2] Fevvers is not just a character within the novel, however, but a clue as to how to read the novel. Fevvers's actions mirror the novel's actions, and the way we respond to her controls our response to the novel. Her slogan teasingly suggests that fact and fiction might be discrete and easily discernible, and to make them so is the project of journalist Jack Walser as he tries to debunk some of Fevvers's mystery. Not only her wings but the story of her life as a child—she is hatched from an egg, grows up in a brothel, and sells herself into willing slavery in order to provide money for her new foster family—gives Walser cause to doubt. Fevvers is a woman who makes a spectacle of herself. Carter called her "Mae West with wings";[3] in *The Sadeian Woman*, as well as in several interviews, Carter expresses her admiration for Mae West's "anarchic freedom" (*SW*, 60), for this "sexually free woman, economically independent, who wrote her own starring vehicles in her early days in the theatre and subsequently exercised an iron hand on her own Hollywood career" (*SW*, 61). Even more than her career, though, Carter admires "the way Mae West controls the audience-response towards herself in her movies."[4] Like Mae West, Fevvers exists to be looked at. Six feet two inches tall, sporting multicolored wings, she makes a virtue of necessity, because it would be hard not to look at Fevvers. In her performance, however, she has complete control over her audience; it may not believe what it sees, but it is still enthralled by the exhibition. As Walser points out, the very limitations of Fevvers's act make it all the more probable that she is what she seems, and yet the paradox, as he recognizes, is that "in a secular age, an authentic miracle must purport to be a hoax, in order to gain credit in the world" (*NC*, 17). Fevvers exploits the uncertainty; she keeps the audience watching because it is never sure whether seeing really *is* believing.

Fevvers controls the gaze of the spectators, but also that of the reader. She is a consummate storyteller, and when she tells her own story, she manipulates both her reader and her material for maximum effect. She provides "proof" of her veracity by giving Walser checkable names and addresses. Lizzie, Fevvers's foster mother, occasionally warns Fevvers away from certain topics, and thus the story she tells seems to be only part of a larger narrative. This, too, contributes a sense of realism to the tale. Yet the story she tells is so full of fantastic events and characters that both Walser and the reader constantly have to revise their opinions and expectations. As in *The Passion of New Eve*, sight is never the sole determination of reality. When Walser describes Fevvers's eyes as "Chinese boxes," he points to the "infinite plurality" in any act of seeing or reading (*NC*, 30). This multiplicity is emphasized by Lizzie's chiming in to Fevvers's narrative with the phrase "Oracular proof. . . . Seeing is believing" (*NC*, 83). This is a punning reference to Shakespeare's *Othello*, in which Othello demands *ocular* proof of Desdemona's infidelity. *Ocular* and *oracular,* of course, mean different things, but although seeing may justify belief, as it does in *Othello*, seeing does not prove anything. Othello is wrong in his judgment of Desdemona, and the ocular proof provides him only with what he expects to see. Lizzie's use of the word *oracular* implies that seeing has as complicated a relation to believing as fact does to fiction. Oracles are notoriously enigmatic, and oracular proof is pretty much an oxymoron. The phrase implies that, in fact, one sees and believes what one wishes to, or what one's history allows.

Not that everyone who sees in the novel has this multiple perspective. As Fevvers's apprenticeship in the brothel as well as in the museum of women monsters shows, looking can be just as reifying as Carter has demonstrated in her earlier novels. The women who sell their bodies are used to being looked at as objects, but despite Fevvers's control over her audience's response, she is not above exhibiting herself if the price is right. When it suits her, Fevvers is an altruist, but for the most part, she looks out for herself. The gifts bestowed on her by adoring fans are put safely in the bank, and she will go to some lengths to procure these gifts, as she does in her encounter with the Grand Duke. Despite the danger in her solitary meeting with him, she sees only the diamonds he has promised her as well as the possibility of further riches to be paid for the evening of entertainment she might be asked to provide. In the middle of the dinner table, the Duke has placed a life-size ice sculpture of Fevvers in full flight, and around the sculpture's neck is the diamond necklace with which he has lured Fevvers to his house. Faced with this vision of herself as a commodity, Fevvers begins to feel uneasy, although she has some responsibility for the way in which he sees her. The sinister nature of the encounter is enhanced by the Duke's weird toys, a trio of clockwork musicians and a collection of jeweled eggs containing far too realistic figures. When Fevvers sees the egg that has a vacant perch, she knows she is to be the Duke's next acquisition, and while she distracts him with a sexual caress, she quickly plans her escape. One of the eggs contains a model of the Trans-Siberian Express, and while the Duke is otherwise engaged, she throws the toy onto the carpet, runs down the platform, and throws herself into the first-class compartment.

This scene contains the most economical moment of fantasy in the novel. In the space of a few sentences, Fevvers is whisked away from the Duke's house to the reality represented by the toy train. Whatever the suspension of disbelief one might have practiced so far, Fevvers's sudden transmigration gives one pause. Readers find themselves in the position that Walser has been in all along with regard to Fevvers's wings, although the wings themselves seem almost prosaic by comparison. The scene is a reminder that this is indeed a fiction, evidence that is far more pointed than any statement the narrative voice could make because the scene engages the reader directly.

On the train across Siberia, Fevvers begins to fade. The vast empti-
ness of the snowy wasteland, like a "blank sheet of fresh paper" (*NC*,
218), deprives Fevvers of her audience, and when she is not seen, she has
no purpose. She becomes sulky, and the dye in her hair and on her wings
loses color. Although she has lost one audience, Fevvers ensures that her
readers will still be focused on her by narrating her trek in the first person. When the train is blown up by outlaws, who escort the travelers to
a shack in the forest, however, the possibility of an audience seems
remote, and Fevvers's broken wing means she can neither perform nor
fly for help. Walser, who had joined the circus as a clown, and whose
love for Fevvers eventually exceeds his desire to prove her a hoax, is
buried in the train wreck. Although he is discovered, he has lost his
memory, which begins to return when he is in the company of a shaman
and his people. Only when Fevvers finds Walser again does she begin to
recover.

Like the landscape in *Heroes and Villains*, the Siberian wilderness provides an opportunity for philosophical and political speculation. Almost
all of the characters whom the travelers encounter are victims of, or
refugees from, political manipulation. Lizzie has been secretly sending
bulletins home from Russia in the diplomatic mailbag, having promised
a gentleman she had met in the British Museum, likely Karl Marx, to
send news to exiled comrades. In the Siberian section of the novel, Lizzie
comes into her own, and her frequent expositions in the face of political
injustices show that she brooks no romantic idealism. Her pragmatism,
indeed, is what keeps the travelers going, although the small group
eventually parts company. The Colonel goes off toward the railroad
track. Mignon, along with her lover, the Princess, and Samson, the
repentant strongman, remain in the Musical Academy of Transbaikalia,
and only Lizzie and Fevvers arrive at the village where Walser is slowly
regaining his memory.

The final chapters are a complex web of images. Sight imagery pre-
dominates as Fevvers begins to recover her looks and her humor in antic-
ipation of finding Walser. Seeing herself in his eyes will, she believes,
restore her to wholeness. Fevvers has another task in mind for Walser.
More than just her beloved, he will be the amanuensis of the "histories of
those women who would otherwise go down nameless and forgotten"
(*NC*, 285). In a soaring speech to Lizzie, Fevvers imagines Walser's role as
helping to alleviate the plight of women in the new century.

The Walser they discover, however, is not yet in full possession of his
faculties. The shaman has taken Walser on as an apprentice, and

although his memory is returning, he now thinks, helped by a regular infusion of hallucinogens dissolved in urine, that those memories are mystical visions. Unfamiliar with the English language, the shaman interprets Walser's snatches of song and his exclamations as visionary ravings. The phrase "Eel pie and mash" (*NC* 256), for example, convinces the shaman that Walser is ready to enter, full-fledged, into his new profession. Walser's experience with the shaman further complicates the apparent dichotomy between fact and fiction. When the facts of Walser's life start to come back to him, he interprets them as fictions, and this interpretation paradoxically makes his memories more real in the shaman's cosmogony, because he depends for his reality on just such visions. When Fevvers arrives in the village, therefore, Walser thinks she is a vision, and because he doesn't immediately apprehend her as real, she feels herself fading. Because his eyes are still tinged with hallucinatory sights, their reflection of her causes her to wonder whether she is indeed fact or fiction. At Lizzie's suggestion, Fevvers reveals her wings, and it is ironic that the sight of those marvelous appendages restores both Fevvers and Walser to reality. Taking on her performing self, Fevvers curtseys to the assembled crowd as she feels their eyes give her new life.

The novel ends with Fevvers's laughter, a laughter that surrounds the globe at the expense of Walser's erroneous belief in her virginity. Having confessed the other tricks she has played on him, she finds it hugely amusing that he has not seen through this one. However, her last sentence, "It just goes to show there's nothing like confidence" (*NC*, 294), goes no distance toward resolving the fact-and-fiction debate. The shaman, too, is associated with confidence, because he has to negotiate between the visions he sees and the demands of his constituents for ocular proof of those visions. When he produces concrete manifestations of the spirits he sees, however, he does not do so out of disbelief in those spirits. The narrator describes the shaman as the "supreme form" (*NC*, 263) of the confidence game because both he and his people have confidence in his integrity. Fevvers's confidence also depends on the belief the audience (and the reader) invests in her, although this does not fix Fevvers's identity as either fact or fiction, but as a negotiation between seer and seen.

The Pleasure of the Text

Fevvers's sexuality is at the crux of the confidence game she has perpetrated on Walser because from the beginning of the novel, her appetites and pleasures are overt, although she has fooled him into thinking that the legend of her inaccessibility is true. During the interview, however, Fevvers exhibits all of the physical language of sexual experience. She flirts, she winks, and she is unembarrassed by sexual matters. Much is made of the number of men who covet her and shower her with gifts, which surely have more than an innocent motive. Her apprenticeship in the brothel is not just an introduction to being looked at, but also an instruction in sexuality, at least as an observer, and that her first role there is as Cupid implies that she has an active role to play in the creation of desire. *Nights at the Circus* certainly has a different relation to desire than does *The Infernal Desire Machines of Doctor Hoffman*, where actualized desire eventually leads to disenchantment and boredom. Whereas Desiderio is not in control of his unconscious fantasies even when they are mirrored back to him, Fevvers seems very much in control of what she wants, including maintaining an aura of mystery. She distinguishes between giving of her "me-ness," which would involve relinquishing her essence, and giving of herself "out of gratitude or in the expectation of pleasure" (*NC*, 280–81). Much of Fevvers's pleasure is involved with being seen, even while she conceals some part of herself. In this, she is like the novel itself, which both reveals and conceals in order to engage the reader's pleasure in interpretation. "Is not the most erotic portion of the body where the garment gapes?"[5] asks Roland Barthes, and the tantalizing gapes in the garment of the text lead to an erotics of reading, not because these gapes can be somehow penetrated, but because they excite layers of surmise.

Barthes writes that when reading is merely an act of consumption, it becomes boring: "to be bored means that one cannot produce the text, open it out, *set it going*."[6] Boredom is a familiar emotion for Carter's characters; Finn, Jewel, and Desiderio all experience it, usually because they are faced with a situation over which they have no control. When Finn, in *The Magic Toyshop*, is at the mercy of Uncle Philip's authority, when Jewel, in *Heroes and Villains*, is given an already constructed role to play by Donally, or when Desiderio is confronted with Doctor Hoffman's manipulation of his unconscious, they are denied any volition. The singularity that leads to boredom is something Carter's novel seeks to avoid by encouraging an interaction between text and reader by means of the plurality of voices, the fluidity of identity, and even the interpretive problems posed by the characters' philosophical questions. Moreover, because this is a novel whose heroine desires and is explicitly desired, eroticism becomes as much a part of reading as eroticism is of her character. The shape of this erotics of reading is far more diffuse than what Rosencreutz, for example, offers Fevvers. His medallion is engraved with a phallus rampant being pulled down to earth by the female rose. His fear of the female is almost as great as his desire to live forever, and on May Day, on the authority of cabalistic calculations, he seeks to sacrifice Fevvers. As in *The Passion of New Eve,* the phallus represents a singular trajectory, but whereas Mother seeks only to reverse this trajectory, *Nights at the Circus* suggests that the multiplicity of the nestled rose petals is a more appropriate model for the feminization of time and narrative.

Walser's speculations about Fevvers's wings concentrate both his and the reader's attention on her body. Her very physicality is emphasized throughout the novel, from her size and the color of her hair to her flatulence and stubbled armpits. Through his writing, Walser wants to reveal to the world Fevvers's body as the humbug that he thinks it is. Walser, however, never writes his reports; in fact, his voice appears only briefly, although in one instance it is to confess his love for Fevvers, apparently aroused by her humiliation of him. Fevvers, too, falls in love with the "unfinished" Walser, remembering, when she sees him, the "vague, imaginary face of desire" (*NC,* 204). Because the whole dynamic of the plot seems to be to bring these two together, it may seem odd that their acquaintance is limited to a night's interview and two other encounters. Fevvers desires desire; she thrives on being adored and looked at, and Walser, by following her tour, proves his adulation. That she describes him as unfinished implies that she sees a role for herself in completing him, although doing so proves to be impossible because his experience with the shaman has changed him irrevocably. Their eventual union is merely sexual, and there is no ecstatic merging of the kind imagined by, for example, Desiderio. Fevvers cannot complete Walser, and Walser feels insufficiently intimate with Fevvers even to call her by her given name. Fevvers's laughter, however, suggests that this failure is no cause for despair; her laughter embraces all who hear it, not to unify them, but to remind them of pleasures still to come.

Crime and Punishment

Although Fevvers can control much of the way people look at her, her exhibitionism sometimes leads her into danger. When Rosencreutz sees her as an angel whose sacrifice will grant him immortality, and the Grand Duke tries to add her to his collection of exotic toys, it is because they confuse the performance with the performer. Fevvers seems to reveal herself completely, although Walser remarks that the anonymity of her dressing room is an indication that some part of her is hidden. On one hand, this implies a realism that adds another facet to the debate between fact and fiction. It implies that there is more to Fevvers than meets the eye, and yet, because she is a character in a novel, there is no more to her than can be seen. On the other hand, however, the Grand Duke and Rosencreutz both have a vision of Fevvers that attempts to fix her identity into a single, static interpretation, and as every aspect of the novel suggests, this is not a fruitful way to look. Of course, Fevvers is always at the mercy of her appearance, and she fears that she might be fixed in that appearance, either by the ministrations of characters such as the Grand Duke and Rosencreutz or even by the "kiss of a magic prince" (NC, 39) such as Walser. In Ma Nelson's brothel, at Madame Schreck's museum, and in the circus, Fevvers trades on the economic value of her wings, but as Lizzie points out, "it's always a symbolic exchange" (NC, 185). No matter how much of Mae West's chutzpah Fevvers exhibits, she still sprouts wings, and doing so gives her only an intermittent power over those who see her.

While Fevvers is hovering between ways of seeing and being seen, there are others in the novel who have even less choice in how they are perceived. Nights at the Circus is a novel of voices; many characters tell their stories and have their stories told. Because the landscape of the Siberian wilderness is so threatening, these stories have a particular urgency. The narratives in this section of the novel all have a didactic political aim and are the stories of people used and abused by political manipulation. Among these narratives, the story of the women's prison clearly shows the dangers of a vision that is motivated by an idée fixe. The imagery of sight and the theme of oppression connect this section to the rest of the novel, although the plot connects it only tangentially. The opening sentence asserts that "no signpost points the way" (NC, 210) to the prison and that no trace remains of the tracks the inhabitants made in getting there. The prison's geographical isolation matches the isolation of this story, which very much stands as a set piece within the novel.

The Countess P., having poisoned her husband without getting caught, decides to create a penitentiary for women who have also killed their husbands but who have been imprisoned for the crime. Using a phrenologist to determine the possibility of each prisoner's salvation, she waits for the women to admit their responsibility for and remorse at their common crime. Not one of them ever does. The Countess P. forces them to build their own jail, a panopticon based on Jeremy Bentham's ideal prison, whose structure ensures the power of the warden through the total visibility of the inmates. Carter's description of the panopticon is so remarkably close to Michel Foucault's in *Discipline and Punish* that she is likely invoking his ideas on the workings of power. A panopticon, as both Carter and Foucault describe it, is a circular honeycomb of cells surrounding a central tower in which the warden sits. Because the inmates are perfectly visible from the tower, but the guard can be seen only intermittently from the cells, the panopticon makes the actual exercise of power unnecessary. Because the prisoners do not always know when they are being observed, they behave as though they always are—in essence, they police themselves. The Countess P. sits in a revolving chair, whose speed is variable, so that the convicts never know when they will come under her scrutiny. Ironically, of course, Countess P. is as much a prisoner as those she watches, and when the prisoners and guards unite to overthrow her, they do so by turning upon her a "united look of accusation" (*NC*, 218).

Both Carter and Foucault describe the cells as "so many small theatres"[7] in which each actor is always visible, and the imagery of performance connects the panopticon to the circus, which also takes place in a round ring with a "still vortex" (*NC*, 107) at its center. As the circus is a microcosm, so is the panopticon, and the similarity between the two is a reminder of the mechanisms of power that seek to control people who are considered abnormal. Like the women who have murdered their husbands, the circus performers are on the fringes of society. Both are controlled by being rendered perfectly visible and therefore are assumed to pose no threat. People who watch the circus are consumers of the performances; the actors in the panopticon are consumed by the eyes of Countess P. As if to make the point more clearly, Carter uses food imagery to describe the prison: its shape is like a doughnut, its cells are like *babas au rhum*, and its structure is like a honeycomb.

The panopticon in *Nights at the Circus* eventually fails because Olga Alexandrovna, whose son Ivan has been tossed from the circus train by Walser, rids herself of guilt and thus refuses the imposition of the prison. Countess P. may consume by watching, but Olga has herself been consumed by the question of her culpability. Having spent three years going over and over the circumstances that led to her killing her brutal husband, she comes to the conclusion that the blame is not hers. With the liberating energy this revelation brings, she begins to take notice of her surroundings, and when the gloved hand of her guard slips through the grill to deliver her food, Olga grasps it. Now, food becomes the means of erotic communication, and when a love note arrives in the hollow center of a roll, she devours the words.

The prisoners and guards hope to found a female utopia, but lest this be seen as Carter's overly romantic solution to women's problems under patriarchy, it is worth noting that the novel severely criticizes all forms of idealism. When Lizzie, the practical anarchist, hears of the female utopia from the Escapee, she wonders what the women will do to boy babies born to the community with the help of the Escapee's donation of sperm: "Feed 'em to the polar bears? To the *female* polar bears?" (*NC*, 240–41). The Escapee receives some harsh words from Lizzie because he believes that with the coming century will come the harmony and perfection of the human soul. Lizzie, however, treats him to a postmodern analysis of his language, calling into question his assumptions about the future, which ignore the problems of the present. For her, it is the past that has created the present, and she feels that the Escapee's concentration on a future perfection ignores the history that has "forged the institutions which create the human nature of the present" (*NC*, 240). That the Escapee eventually becomes the business manager for the Colonel, whose idea of perfection rests wholly with the dollar bill, makes an ironic comment on the Escapee's notion of the perfectibility of the human soul. Even Fevvers herself should be viewed with a skeptical eye. Although she is supposed to be a portent of the coming century, in which "no woman will be bound down to the ground" (*NC*, 25), she is nonetheless a creature who could exist only in the realm of fiction, and a reminder that this idealistic time has not yet come.

Chaos, Time, and History

Like postmodernism, chaos theory examines problems associated with order, origins, linearity, and turbulence. Both look at the way in which the world is structured and call into question past theories and discoveries, and if postmodernism does so using literary, rather than physical, tropes, it is nonetheless trying to ask readers to consider how we know and what we know of the world. Carter's interest in both time and the position of the reader, as well as the episodic style that calls into question linearity and cause and effect, aligns her texts not only with postmodernism but also with recent scientific theories that seek to examine these issues in the physical world. Both postmodernism and chaos theory are concerned with what Katherine Hayles calls a "denaturing process,"[8] which she explains as the "realization that what has always been thought of as the essential, unvarying components of human experience are not natural facts of life but social constructions."[9] This would not be news to a reader of Carter's fiction, but *Nights at the Circus* lends itself particularly to an analysis that takes the theory of chaos into account because of the theory's emphasis on disorder and its complication of time.

Fevvers's act defies the laws of gravity either because she is what she seems or because she has to pretend to be what she seems in order to maintain the hoax. Such is the paradox of the novel as she and Lizzie travel the world while Fevvers is loved and pursued by figures such as Edward VII and Toulouse-Lautrec. Despite her star status, Fevvers's physique causes some observers to see her as a freak and a marginal figure, even though she participates in central historical events with historically verifiable characters. These stories, such as Fevvers's being the object of the peculiar erotic fantasies of the rich and famous, do not, of course, appear in the history books. *Nights at the Circus* is a historiographic metafiction in that the novel critically examines events that may have contributed to, but have been effaced from, transcriptions of historical events. The novel suggests that although these are very specific historical moments, they are other than those presented in official histories. The novel combines official histories with individual stories that may be as believable or as unbelievable as official history itself.

Nights at the Circus takes place in 1899, "on the cusp," as the narrator says, "of the modern age. . . . in those last bewildering days before history, that is, history as we know it, that is, white history, that is, European history, that is, Yanqui history . . . extended its tentacles to grasp the entire globe" (*NC*, 265). The date is a very specific transition, a moment in which time seems to stand still because although the past has led to this moment, nothing can explain how it is going to lead into the uncertain future. Carter's narrator responds to the uncertainty of the future by proposing to stop time altogether. She or he imagines that if a global plebiscite were taken among all the inhabitants of the world, there would be universal concurrence that "the whole idea of the twentieth century, or any other century at all for that matter, was a rum notion," and that if this plebiscite were acted upon, "the twentieth century would have forthwith ceased to exist, . . . and time, by popular consent, would have stood still" (*NC*, 265).

The novel explores the notion of a continuing present as a way of making time stand still, thereby limiting the uncertainty of the future.

When Carter's novels resist closure by positing a future world, that world seems pretty grim. Were one to break a rule of interpretation and imagine what happens to characters after the novels' ends, there would be little cause for optimism. *Nights at the Circus* suggests a future that, to the reader, is already past, although we too are at the end of a century and might find some similarities in the attitudes of fear and excitement that attend the coming of a new one. Fevvers and Lizzie are ambivalent about their new century. On the one hand, Fevvers may be the portent of the "New Age in which no woman will be bound down to the ground" (*NC*, 25). On the other, both Lizzie and Fevvers speculate that Beauty dreams the twentieth century and comment on "how frequently she weeps" (*NC*, 86).

In their dressing room, Fevvers and Lizzie keep a clock that they call, appropriately enough, Father Time. Through the clock, they can control time, and the clock's hands always stand at midnight or noon, "the still hour in the centre of the storm of time" (*NC*, 29). But when they lose the clock in the train accident in Siberia, time ceases to be uniform and becomes relative. For example, what has seemed merely a week to Lizzie and Fevvers as they wander through the Siberian snow has been enough time for Walser to learn a whole new language and to grow a full and lengthy beard. In their travels, Lizzie and Fevvers meet Siberian tribes-people who do not measure time mechanically but rather judge it by the diurnal cycles of light and dark and the passing of the seasons: "they inhabited a temporal dimension which did not take history into account. They were a-historic. Time meant nothing to them" (*NC*, 265). The tribespeople inhabit, in a sense, a perpetual *now*, enacting rituals drawn from their mythology, whose importance is not gained from the *pastness* of the past but from its continuing *present*. Every year, the tribespeople sacrifice a bear whose spirit, they believe, will carry messages to the dead. Although the ritual is ancient, the people have no conception of its antiquity because they have no means of differentiating between past, present, and future. As the narrator tells us, death itself is "not precisely mortal" (*NC*, 258) because the people assume a perpetual cycle in which the bear, though dead, will be up and around again in no time, only to be killed again at an appropriate moment in the cycle.

The concern with time and the possibility of a field in which all space-time can exist simultaneously obviously contradicts our phenomenological experience of time, as well as physical laws. In true metafictional fashion, we as readers are faced with the paradox of reading forward in accordance with the progress of time while simultaneously looking back to the past. We recognize, too, that our reading is what makes the novel always present to us as we read. In a sense, through reading, we can defy physical laws as Fevvers defies time and gravity. Walser's experience with time during his interview with Fevvers is a good example of this process, because he is the reader's emissary in the fictional world, and he "reads" Fevvers as though he were reading a novel. Toward the end of his interview with Fevvers, after Big Ben has perplexed him by striking midnight three times over the course of the evening, time suddenly seems to jump forward to six o'clock. As the chimes are striking, Walser feels as a reader might feel at the end of a novel, as though the room had been "plucked out of its everyday, temporal continuum, had been held for a while above the spinning world and was now—dropped back into space" (*NC*, 87).

In the face of the chaotic, unknowable future, the novel seems, on one level at least, to draw comfort from the idea of a continuing present that we know and therefore think we can control. Such control has arguably been the task of the traditional history that seeks to fix the past in writing, demarcate it, and put it tidily away. In the novel's imaginative rejection of physical laws, *Nights at the Circus* seems to suggest a way of looking at history that on one hand emphasizes connections and on the other, discontinuities and ruptures. In the physical world, we cannot stop time, even if we choose to ignore it. The second law of thermodynamics tells us that although the energy in the universe is constant, the availability of this energy is always decreasing, moving toward dissipation, because entropy, or disorder, is always increasing. Because of this, as Paul Davies explains in *The Cosmic Blueprint*, physicists have posited that the "universe as a whole is engaged in *unidirectional change*, an asymmetry often symbolized by an imaginary 'arrow of time,' pointing from past to future."[10] Given an entropic universe, it is understandable that fictions such as Carter's suggest the possibility of ignoring, and therefore stopping, time. If we were to ignore time in the physical world, we would still grow old, however strong our conviction to the contrary; but fictional characters, obviously, do not age in our sense, and thus for them, entropy does not exist.

In *The Passion of New Eve*, the entropic world is evidenced by the civil war, and Evelyn predicts that the chaotic city is steadily moving toward dissipation. Mother certainly seems to be exploiting theories of chaos in her transformation of Evelyn into Eve; Mother's attempt to feminize time is an attempt to make time run backward rather than continuing on as a phallic arrow. In *Nights at the Circus*, the clowns are the ones who symbolize the end of the world. When they explain their craft to Walser, the clowns emphasize that they have chosen to be what they are and that they create themselves by choosing their individual masks. Yet choice is not enough to assuage the misery, humiliation, and despair that is the clowns' lot in life. The clowns' creation of masks does not allow them the "vertiginous sense of freedom" (*NC*, 103) that Walser finds when he puts on his own clown face. Buffo and the others tell Walser that underneath their makeup is nothing but absence. The violence and pain that characterizes their performance is real, and although the spectators may laugh, their laughter merely implicates them in the "celebration of the primal slime" (*NC*, 125). The clowns' dance in the Siberian wasteland is an invocation to destruction. The outlaws who blow up the circus train do so because they believe that Fevvers will soon be married to the Prince of Wales and, as a member of the royal family, will be able convince Queen Victoria to persuade the Tsar to pardon them. The ruse discovered, they are sunk in gloom, and the travelers fear for their lives. Lizzie sends the clowns to cheer them up, but the ensuing performance is a dance of death. The clowns invoke entropy by dancing "tomorrows into yesterdays" (*NC*, 243), and when the storm that sweeps over them clears, neither the outlaws nor the clowns remain. They have succumbed to the inevitable conclusion to entropy: the end of the world. Although the clowns are a reminder that entropy is increasing, the result of their performance is the freedom of the travelers, who have, for the moment, survived the dance of death. Their survival raises one of the optimistic arguments of chaos theory, which suggests that in a system as complex as the universe, the entropy of limited systems can be reversed for long periods. Nature, apparently disordered and chaotic, is creative and can organize itself into complex forms that "borrow" against the energy available in the universe to create high concentrations of energy such as the human body, a tree, or a flower. Chaos, contrary to our "common sense" view of the term, is never entirely random because it shows repeated, discernible patterns, even if these are unpredictable. Cause and effect, far from being the relation expressed in linear equations and in traditional representations of history, are, in fact, not linear at all: *small* causes can create *large* effects. The image often used to illustrate this notion is the butterfly whose beating wings in one part of the world can cause storms in another. In *Nights at the Circus*, the Colonel's publicity linking Fevvers to the Prince of Wales causes the outlaws to blow up the train, and the consequences of this act lead to even more complexity. The science of chaos, as Katherine Hayles sees it, "provides a new way of thinking about order, conceptualising it not as a totalized condition but as the replication of symmetries that also allows for asymmetries and unpredictabilities."[11]

One of the phenomena of chaos theory is the "strange attractor," which Katherine Hayles describes as "any point within an orbit that seems to attract the system to it."[12] Like the midpoint of a pendulum's swing or a rock in the middle of a flowing river, a strange attractor is the point at which a new order is precipitated out of the turbulence of the old; it is the point to which the system keeps returning. Fevvers is perhaps the best example of this concept. As Joanne M. Gass has written, Fevvers's presence in any institution anticipates its demise.[13] Shortly after she begins to pose as the Winged Victory at Ma Nelson's, business declines. When Madame Schreck tries to cheat Fevvers out of the money she has earned in the museum of women monsters, she hooks the Madame onto a chandelier, where she is later found dead. The circus loses some of its members to disaster and others to defection even before the ill-fated trip across Siberia.

To some extent, Fevvers is like the clowns because she always seems to be the center of a whirlwind of destruction. That she is herself subject to entropy is clear from her encounters with what Carter in an interview called "mad scientists": Rosencreutz and the Grand Duke.[14] As Carter puts it, "Each time she encounters a mad scientist Fevvers gets away, and each time she loses a little more of herself."[15] She loses some of her feathers escaping Rosencreutz, her sword fleeing the Grand Duke; and in the train wreck, she loses the gloss on her appearance. Out of the destruction, however, new orders are created just as, according to chaos theory, ordered systems may arise that concentrate the energy of an otherwise entropic universe. The women in Ma Nelson's brothel move on to other, happy, lives. Fevvers is instrumental in helping Madame Schreck's victims discover talents and occupations other than exhibiting themselves as freaks. Fevvers saves Mignon and fosters her relationship with the Princess and presides over a number of other changing orders. Whether Fevvers is active in the changes or not, they seem to flow around her.

The link between Fevvers and the novel suggests that *Nights at the Circus* itself could be described as a strange attractor that precipitates new orders. This is not surprising given Carter's characteristic polemicism. By combining postmodernism with theories drawn from the new physics, she seems to suggest that even the smallest cause—reading, for example—may create large effects and that new orders can be found in the turbulence of the old. Chaos theory is remarkably optimistic in this way, and *Nights at the Circus* echoes that optimism.

Boundaries and Thresholds

In Siberia, the travelers are in limbo. The white landscape, compared in the novel to a blank page, provides a place for writings and rewritings. In this landscape, nothing is absolute; everything is in flux. The Maestro gets his pupils; the Princess finds her voice; and Walser finds, if not himself, then at least *a* self. This state of flux is perhaps why the idealism proposed by the Escapee, the women's utopia, and even Samson the strongman, however admirable, seems to be static. Lizzie is all for change, although it is not the change of the moment she yearns for, but a reconfiguration of the "anvil of history" (*NC*, 240). Just as time is on the threshold of a new era, so Siberia is a liminal place of possibilities.

While Siberia may be the most obvious, the numerous images connected to liminality suggest that change can happen when the traditional boundaries of knowledge are questioned and crossed. A limen is a threshold; it marks a moment of transition from one state to another. Part of a rite of passage, for example, includes a liminal period in which the person undergoing the rite "passes through a cultural realm that has few or none of the attributes of the past or coming state."[16] Walser is the most obvious example of such a person, because although his state when he is with the shaman has *some* of the attributes of Walser's past life, he cannot understand them. When he does return to self-consciousness, neither he nor Fevvers can see what he will become. He does, however, learn what it is to be afraid, a state that, at the beginning of the novel, he had never experienced. Now he knows what it is to fear the "loss of the beloved" (*NC*, 292–93).

Fevvers also exemplifies such an in-between state. Not only is the debate about her slogan never resolved, but as part human, part bird, she raises even more difficult questions about what it means to be human. Other characters who serve the same function are those in Madame Schreck's museum. Madame Schreck collects for her brothel women whom she designates as monsters, although the men who use the brothel's services might be similarly described. Both the women and their clients exist on a fragile boundary between the natural and unnatural. They are grotesques in the sense that they make the familiar unfamiliar, and they arouse both fascination and fear. If Fevvers and her colleagues are perversions of nature, then so are the circus animals who exhibit human reason, although they are more likely to arouse wonder and admiration than fear. When patrons enter the circus, they leave their fur coats in a cloakroom, leaving behind "the skin of [their] own beastliness so as not to embarrass the beasts with it" (*NC*, 105). The beasts, however, can take care of themselves: the literate apes write their own contract, Sybil the Mystic Pig can not only spell but prophesy, and the tigers can waltz.

The animal and the human, and the human and the monstrous, are combined and mixed up to an extent that would appear to presage chaos. The reader, like the audience at the circus, must acknowledge that there is no clear separation between the animal and the human, so what it means to have an identity in the first place is a troubled but unresolved question. That there are so many unresolved dichotomies puts the reader in the position of the initiate in a rite of passage. With characteristic didactic flair, Carter makes her reader see her point. Like the liminal space of the initiate, the novel provides a place that is in-between what Carter may hope are the reader's two realities, the latter of which may change with the intervention of the novel's ideas.

Conclusion: Absent Mothers

Mothers in Carter's novels are conspicuous by their absence. Lizzie is the most sustained maternal figure so far, and even in *Wise Children*, whose story is very much concerned with origins, what drives the narrative is a search for paternity. Carter said in an interview that houses in her novels took the place of mothers;[17] however, because the houses, particularly in her early fiction, are rotting structures that have seen better days, her comment does not illuminate the problem. Apart from Joseph's mother, who is presented as a figure to be avoided, and Mrs. Boulder in *Several Perceptions*, biological mothers are either dead or on the sidelines. Maternal figures do have a place in the novels, although that place is highly ambiguous. Margaret, who replaces the dead mother in *The Magic Toyshop*, is tender and loving, but she is very much a victim of Philip's tyranny. It is significant that Margaret has no voice, and when she finds it at the end of the novel, her voice is used to express her self-sacrifice. We cannot help but assume that she has given herself up to the flames to save Finn's and Melanie's lives. In *The Infernal Desire Machines*, Mama is a nurturing and sexual woman, but she is also prepared to comply with tradition and participate in Desiderio's murder and cannibalism. Albertina's mother is dead and horribly preserved by Doctor Hoffman, and the sexual acrobatics of the caged lovers do not, it would seem, result in pregnancy. Images of *rebirth* pervade the novel, but each rebirth is almost a parthenogenesis. Desiderio's own mother is a degraded figure whom he remembers in two ways, either as ferociously sexual with her clients or as atoning for her sins with the nuns. She falls, therefore, into the clichéd representation of woman as whore or madonna. Mother is a central figure in *The Passion of New Eve*, although with her eight surgically attached breasts, she is a technological rather than biological marvel. Eve, too, is born of technology, not of woman, and the Mother she finds at the end of the novel is dying and mad.

It is interesting that Carter's criticism of the symbols used to keep women as passive objects rather than active subjects ignores maternity as a source of power. In the novels, maternity is shown to be very much in the service of the patriarchy. In *The Sadeian Woman*, Carter describes the pornographic representation of intercourse as one in which the male aspires and the woman is passive: "Between [woman's] legs lies nothing but zero, the sign for nothing, that only becomes something when the male principle fills it with meaning" (*SW*, 4). This is a description of pornography, not of conception, but because the sexual act is part of both, such a description would seem to rob motherhood of all but a moment of passivity. In the Freudian model, on which Carter's iconography draws for both criticism and symbolism, the woman has a baby to replace the symbolically lost phallus. One can hardly imagine Carter taking such a line without a fight. The return to mother in a number of the novels, however, is modeled on strictly Oedipal lines: mother is eroticized, but as such is clearly a threat because of the social interdiction against incest.

The pregnant woman, however, is a powerful figure, and Carter uses pregnant woman characters as a way of cheating closure, because pregnancy is a state of becoming and potential. The characters who are pregnant at the end of Carter's novels are independent, if alone. In *Heroes and Villains,* Marianne firms her resolve to take control of the Barbarians after her initial terror at her condition. Eve, whose pregnancy is guessed at by both Mother and Lilith, wishes to be borne on the ocean to the "place of birth" (*NE*, 191) and sets out with independent resolve. Emily, pregnant with Honeybuzzard's child in *Shadow Dance*, is self-possessed as well as being a clear alternative to the masochism exhibited by Ghislaine. *Wise Children* ends with the pregnant Tiffany's rejecting her weak-kneed partner, Tristram. In each case, the pregnant women are in control and suggest both narrative potential and female strength.

Fevvers's origins contribute to her being a mythic creature. She was hatched, as her feathered appendages make clear, and although this assures her paternity, at least for Walser, who or what laid the egg is a mystery. Nonetheless, Lizzie, who adopted Fevvers as a foundling, is as consistent and as powerful a maternal figure as appears in Carter's novels. *Nights at the Circus* has a postmodern regard for history and its problematic relation to narrative. Because the novel takes place on the cusp of a new century, and Fevvers is the child of the new age, the characters are concerned with a future that is the reader's historical past. Not only public but private history is also considered in *Nights at the Circus*, and were Fevver's origins made clear, they would be the only moment of singularity in a novel brimming with multiplicity. As one critic has suggested, the literary tactics of postmodernism—indeterminacy, open-endedness, and fluidity—are in opposition to the biological fact of motherhood, which "operates under the signature of the real."[18] Although it would seem improbable for Carter to be in any way on the side of patriarchal structures, she does seem to degrade biological motherhood in much the same way as reproductive technology is striving to remove women from the realm of childbearing. As a self-professed materialist, Carter's omission is striking. Although the issues of maternity and paternity will become themes in *Wise Children*, it is interesting that Carter creates both a strong adoptive and an absent biological mother in *Nights at the Circus*. In Carter's defense, perhaps, it is possible to say that her multiplicity does provide spaces within which the mother can speak, if only to critique her absence.

Chapter Eight
What You Will: *Wise Children*

"Only untimely death is a tragedy"[1] says Dora Chance, the narrator of *Wise Children* (1991), and her statement lends a particular poignancy to reading Carter's last novel, which was published in the same year she discovered she had cancer. *Wise Children* is, however, Carter's most ribald and wry novel. Twin sisters Dora and Nora Chance are showgirls whose philosophy is that the show must go on, and with the more dancing and singing, the better. "I refuse point-blank to play in tragedy" (*WC*, 153), Dora writes, but however comic in structure and story, the laughter *Wise Children* provokes is ironic and worldly-wise. Salman Rushdie describes the novel's humor as a "deadly cheeriness. It cackles gaily as it impales the century upon its jokes."[2]

Dramatis Personae

Dora and Nora Chance are the illegitimate offspring of Shakespearean actor Melchior Hazard, who himself has a twin brother, Peregrine. While Melchior denies his paternity, Peregrine supports the sisters and becomes their surrogate father. Dora chronicles over 100 years of Hazard and Chance family history, and because both branches of the family are in show business, she charts the changing fads and fashions in the entertainment industry as well. The novel takes place over one day, April 23, the shared birthday of the Chance sisters, the Hazard brothers, and Shakespeare. Dora and Nora are celebrating 75 years; Melchior and Peregrine, 100: in the course of the day, while Dora and Nora wait to go to their father's gala birthday ball, Dora unravels the complicated web of their lives. The novel includes a "Dramatis Personae," a handy reference guide to the genealogy of the cast, for familial relations are by no means what they seem. Paternity is everywhere in dispute, although maternity, too, is surrounded in some mystery. The "natural" daughters of Melchior, Dora and Nora never knew their mother, who died at their birth. They are raised by the woman who ran the boardinghouse for down-at-the-heel actors where their mother was a housemaid, and although they call the woman Grandma and take her name as their own, she may or may not be a blood relative. All the twins know of their mother is her name, Kitty, and what they know of their birth comes entirely from what Grandma Chance has told them, although Grandma's own history is tantalizingly taboo. Grandma is a naturist, a vegetarian with a penchant for boiled cabbage, and a believer in the pain of cut flowers. She likes a tipple of crème de menthe liqueur, in which she is obliged by Peregrine, who, when his fortunes are high, arrives to visit his nieces bearing exotic gifts and crates of crème de menthe. Having been asked by Melchior to acknowledge the twins publicly as his own, Peregrine becomes Dora and Nora's sugar daddy. He sends them money for dancing lessons, takes them on excursions, performs wonderful magic tricks, and makes every visit seem like Christmas. He has, however, little tolerance for boredom: "life had to be a succession of small treats or else he couldn't see the point" (*WC*, 61). Although he is much loved by his nieces, his presence in their lives is only intermittent.

Dora and Nora's career on the stage begins when they play birds in a pantomime at the age of 12, and by the time the twins reach their 16th birthdays, they are old pros. As identical twins, they are a star turn in the music hall, and they become worldly-wise in matters of both performance and sexuality. When they are asked to perform in Melchior's musical tribute to Shakespeare, *What! You Will?* (a title whose punctuation is never the same twice), they and the review become so successful that the cast is hired en masse to film a Hollywood version of *A Midsummer Night's Dream*. The film is a terrible flop, not least because the sexual acrobatics performed offscreen by most of the cast distracts them from the business at hand. Once Dora and Nora return to England, they find that fashions are changing, and the demand for dancers has diminished. They end their careers playing in nude reviews.

Despite the rise and fall of their fortunes, a long list of former lovers, the death of Grandma Chance and the presumed death of Peregrine, their father's lack of recognition, two world wars, and a host of other tragic events, Dora's narration is philosophically upbeat. "Let other pens dwell on guilt and misery" (*WC*, 163), Dora quotes from Jane Austen's *Mansfield Park*; like Austen, Dora concentrates less on national and international events than she does on domestic ones. According to Grandma Chance, wars are the revenge of old men on young ones because "they can't stand the competition" (*WC*, 28). When the bombs fall during World War I, she berates the sky because she knows the old men "hated women and children worst of all" (*WC*, 29). Dora's is an unofficial history, one that the old men might consider illegitimate, although many things of which these old men might approve are eliminated from, or parodied by, Dora's narrative. Not that legitimate—that is, officially sanctioned—history doesn't impinge on the story, but Dora refuses to treat it without irony. The novel does begin, however, with the suggestion of personal tragedy that no irony can efface: the disappearance and possible suicide of Dora and Nora's godchild, Tiffany. She and Tristram Hazard, Melchior's son by his third wife, host a live game show, but on a special birthday tribute to Tristram's father, Tiffany appears unscripted in an Ophelia-like trance. Her feet bleeding from a long walk in stiletto heels, she carries handfuls of flowers and sings as she descends the studio staircase. It becomes clear that she is pregnant, but Tristram, who feels he is not ready to become a father, has rejected her. When the police call to say that the body of a young woman has been found in the Thames, it seems as though the worst has happened. *Wise Children* is a comedy, and it is clear that there will be a happy ending, but this opening scene raises recurring themes and, as it turns out, repeats family history.

Wise Children has much to say about families, not all of it pleasant. Dead and rejected mothers, absent fathers, and nasty siblings provide the impetus for much of the plot. As is often the case in Carter's fiction, though, personal experience has a broader symbolic function. Here, literary culture is also constructed as a family, and Shakespeare is at its head. As a writer, Dora has to come to terms with her *literary* fathers as well as her biological one, and her illegitimacy as a daughter is paralleled by her position as a woman writer who has few literary mothers. Although Dora yearns for acknowledgment from her father, she does not use his voice to write her memoirs, because unlike Melchior, she wants to tell her own story rather than repeating the words of someone else's. At the end of the novel, Tiffany is discovered alive and well, but rejects Tristram's offer of marriage. Her baby will be the continuation of the Hazard clan, and her pregnancy is a way of resisting novelistic closure. Dora and Nora also become adoptive mothers of a twin boy and girl who are Melchior's grandchildren. Dora does not provide the circumstances of their birth because these are, she says, outside the realm of comedy, but here too is a indication that the imaginative process will continue. Nora suggests that no matter what these babies are told about their parents, "they'll make up their own romance out of it" (*WC*, 230).

Family and Other Romances

The title of the novel gives rise to speculation about just what it is that makes a child wise. Knowledge of one's paternity is the condition given in the epigraph, "It's a wise child that knows its own father," although were this indeed true, there would be few wise children in the novel. Nora's comment about the adopted twins suggests that perhaps wisdom is to be gained from the knowledge of how one constructs one's family, a family that in Dora's case includes her literary as well as her biological forebears. Walking home from the birthday party, Dora suggests to Nora that their father looked "two-dimensional" and was "too kind, too handsome, too repentant" (*WC*, 230). Nora's response is to wonder whether they have not been making him up all along and to suppose him a "collection of our hopes and dreams and wishful thinking" (*WC*, 230). One assumption behind the epigraph is echoed by Dora's contention that " 'father' is a hypothesis, but 'mother' is a fact" (*WC*, 223). A wise child, then, would have to engage in an intellectual endeavor to know his or her father, whereas the certainty of maternity, it is implied, needs no exploration. In strictly biological terms, maternity is hardly disputable. Within the context of the novel, however, Dora's is not an entirely satisfactory assertion. The practice of mothering and fathering need not be biologically determined, as is clear from the adoptive parents in the novel. Whether adoptive or biological, parents and children are subject to each other's dreams and wishful thinking, and the relationship may take on any or all of the genres of tragedy, comedy, or romance.

Dora points out that the one fixed point in their family history is their paternal grandmother, Estella. Because nothing is known of their biological mother, Dora and Nora focus their curiosity about their origins on their father's family, whose fortunes are intimately tied to the Shakespeare plays in which the family members star. For example, Melchior's father, Ranulph, meets Estella while they are performing *King Lear*, in which she plays Cordelia to his Lear. His sons appear to have been fathered by another actor, Cassius Booth, during a production of *Hamlet* in which Estella plays the prince and Cassius plays Horatio. Ten years later, on the opening night of *Othello*, Ranulph catches the reunited lovers in bed, and no longer able to distinguish between art and life, kills them and then himself. The family descendants are as much the children of Shakespearean theater as they are of their biological parents.

Peregrine and Melchior dislike each other almost from birth. After their parents' death, the boys are to be raised by a stern aunt, but Peregrine escapes into the wilds of Manhattan, while Melchior is taken to live with his aunt in Scotland. They enter, in fact, different literary genres. Melchior recites his father's roles as he lies in bed at night, and when his aunt insists that Melchior enter the clergy, he steals out of the house and heads for London. Dora describes Peregrine, on the other hand, in the language of "pulp romance" (*WC*, 30). His is a picaresque life, full of adventures and tall tales. By the time the brothers meet again, many years later, Peregrine is an explorer and a wanderer, while Melchior is on his way to becoming a famous actor. The enmity between them never quite dissipates; indeed, it is quietly perpetuated by Peregrine's sleeping with all of Melchior's wives, making at least one of them pregnant.

Although framed in a comic story, family relations are at best strained and at worst cruel. Under the circumstances, it seems odd that Dora's tone is consistently cheerful, although she says that there are limits to laughter's power. Despite the jokes and the bawdy humor, and despite Dora's insistence that she will not perform in a tragedy, much of what happens between family members *is* tragic. Comedy, as Dora says, is "tragedy that happens to *other* people" (*WC*, 213), and so the boundaries between the two genres are always shifting. Dora and Nora are able to put a good face on dreadful events, but the tragedy of their father's treatment of them is hardly a laughing matter. Melchior's denial of his 13-year-old daughters when Peregrine takes them to their father's Brighton dressing room causes the girls considerable grief, and Melchior's later crumbs of affection sprinkled throughout their lives seem poor compensation. At the party that closes the novel, Dora and Peregrine end up in bed together, and she remembers that on the day she and her sister were rejected by her father, she was first seduced by her uncle. The narrative of that day is silent about the seduction, but even if this is meant to be consolation for the father's rejection, it is a peculiar one. When Lynde Court burns down, Melchior is more concerned with losing his pasteboard crown, his one memento of his father, than he is with the safety of his wife and children. It therefore seems a mystery why Dora and Nora continue to seek his affection as it becomes apparent that he is selfish, narcissistic, and melodramatic. They do want his love and recognition; in fact, he is their first romantic attachment, their first crush, and the object of their fantasies all of their lives.

An absent parent may well be an idealized parent; both Dora and Nora have a fantasized relationship to Melchior in which he is their primary object of love. Each sister secretly keeps a photograph of him in her underwear drawer, and in appearance Melchior seems to be the perfect object for a schoolgirl crush. He is handsome and famous, and when war breaks out, he joins the air force and becomes a war hero. His little bits of affection leave his daughters hungry for more, and so they are willing to be the mascots in his Hollywood film, even though during the production he takes the opportunity to deny his paternity in public. Peregrine lavishes affection on his nieces, but his excesses, welcome as they are, still happen only occasionally and also leave Dora and Nora wanting more. Conversely, their relations with Grandma can be strained and sometimes painful, because Dora and Nora are sure Grandma will always be there. Because she is not an exotic treat, they take her affection for granted.

Peregrine's daughters, Saskia and Imogen, think that Melchior is their father, although they treat him just as thoughtlessly as he treats them. On their 21st birthday, when he makes an ill-timed announcement that he is going to marry his Cordelia, Saskia's school friend, and will therefore no longer be able to support his daughters financially, they smash the crockery. They then take their anger out on their mother, Atalanta, by forcing her to sign away all of her assets. When she falls, or perhaps is pushed, down the stairs and ends up in a wheelchair, Saskia and Imogen simply abandon Atalanta to the sympathies of the Chance sisters. At Melchior's party, Saskia's poisoned birthday cake, a model of the Globe Theater, is to be her final revenge on her father for never, she believes, having loved her.

However, relations within families that spring up by chance are much less troubled. The makeshift family in which Dora and Nora grow up, although not without conflict, avoids the kind of viciousness inspired by the legitimate families. Grandma creates a family "out of whatever came to hand" (*WC*, 35), and the twins continue the tradition as they grow older. Theirs is primarily a female household, thanks to absent fathers and husbands. Not only do Dora and Nora live with their father's first wife, but they provide for the daughter and granddaughter of the housemaid who used to look after them. Neither twin marries, despite a succession of lovers, but like Grandma, they create their own family "by sheer force of personality" (*WC*, 35).

The Hazards and the Chances seem opposite in every way. The Hazards are wealthy and privileged, their careers are associated with the elite culture of Shakespearean drama, and even when they perform in television commercials, they do so as theatrical royalty. The Chances,

born on the wrong side of the blanket, and living on the wrong side of
the Thames, have fortunes tied to the rise and fall of popular taste. In
their prime, the Chances are sought after and comfortable, but as they
age, they have to sell off the memorabilia of their youth to pay the gas
bills. Despite the differences in the family fortunes, the words "hazard"
and "chance" are so similar that they are defined in terms of one
another. Both imply an unknown or undetermined cause, and each can
denote a risk or accident. Hazard, however, also implies danger in a way
that chance does not. The Hazard line is the male line, and the confusion attending paternity arguably leads to much of the ill feeling
between family members. The similar meanings of the names, however,
raises the point that these two oppositions may not be as different as
they first appear. Dora makes much of her illegitimacy, and the word
"bastard" appears more often and in more contexts than any other word
in the novel. Yet her narrative, a performance in itself, is as complex and
as cultured as the family she feels has rejected her. Because Shakespearean theater in the novel is the province of the legitimate branch of
the family, it is interesting that Dora's memoirs have five chapters, par-
alleling the five acts of Shakespeare's plays. While their father and
grandfather follow the road of the Bard, Dora and Nora actually live on
Bard Road, number 49. One of the points Carter seems to be making is
that Shakespeare has more in common with illegitimate, working-class,
populist entertainers such as the Chance sisters than with those who
treat him with idolatry.

Dora has learned her second vocation, as a writer, from an author she
meets on the set of the disastrous Hollywood production of *A Midsummer Night's Dream*. Ross "Irish" O'Flaherty gives Dora "Culture" because
he cannot afford to buy her a mink. A practical woman, she accepts his
gift of an alphabetical education in the arts and in return breaks his
heart: "Fair exchange is no robbery" (*WC*, 13), she maintains. While
Ranulph, Melchior, and their fans and hangers-on are extolling the
genius of the poet "who knew the truth about us all and spoke those
universal truths in every phrase" (*WC*, 135), Dora and Nora are trying
to pay the electricity bills, and they realize that what lies behind the
Hazards' exaltation of the Bard is greed and vanity. From the beginning
of the novel, culture is portrayed as an industry, and actors' bodies are
units of exchange. Ranulph may have felt a spiritual call to spread the
word of Shakespeare, but Melchior is really only interested in spreading
his own fame and reaping the profits. In the long run, "our sweated
labour = your bit of fun" (*WC*, 142) applies as much to the Hazards as

to the Chances, and it applies as much to sexual exchange as it does to strutting and fretting upon the stage.

Neither Dora nor her sister is a shrinking violet when it comes to sex, and like Fevvers, each is willing to sell what she has for material reward. Dora is nothing if not pragmatic when it comes to this arrangement and is willing to pay off "an instalment on [her] squirrel jacket" (*WC*, 97) even when she finds her benefactor repulsive. Stockings, fur coats, and flowers all arrive at Bard Road from men who keep such extravagances from their wives. The Hazard line is consumed by mammon on a rather larger scale. Melchior's greed and lust makes his Hollywood debut a flop, although later his version of *A Midsummer Night's Dream* becomes the subject of Ph.D. theses, whose authors request interviews from Dora and Nora. While Atalanta cackles over what she calls the "final degeneration of the House of Hazard" (*WC*, 9), the television program *Lashings of Lolly* hosted by Tristram, there are similarities between his performance in the game show and his father's performance in drama. In fact, reminiscent of his grandfather, whose performances in the colonies often took place on grounds recently vacated by evangelicals, Tristram announces his game show in the "voice of an ecstatic" (*WC*, 11). Sex and money seem to combine in Dora's narrative to flatten out differences between elite and popular culture, and when Dora finds that Shakespeare's head adorns the 20-pound note, she is shocked to discover that he has "turned into actual currency" (*WC*, 191), although she has been in no doubt about his metaphorical status as currency all along.

Dora's own writing partakes of both the elite and the popular, and she is as conversant with the style and speech of both sides of the Thames as she is with music-hall jokes and Shakespearean plots. Introducing the reader to her word processor and filing system at the beginning of the novel, she points out the card indexes that contain the histories of both the right- and the left-hand sides of the family. But the wind blowing outside, the kind that "blows everything topsy-turvey" (*WC*, 3), seems ready to mix everything up, and as the narrative proceeds and the complexities of the family are revealed, it would seem that the wind has had its way. Dora's narrative, however, has more to it than making a mélange of the oppositions between cultures. Although female characters often tell their own stories in Carter's short fiction, Dora is the only sustained first-person female narrator in Carter's novels. That the legitimacy of various kinds of art is raised as a theme in such a context is not surprising, because Dora is not only the illegitimate daughter of a Shakespearean actor; indeed, as a woman writer, she is also the illegitimate daughter of the Western literary tradition. Like Carter herself, Dora acknowledges a debt to her literary forebears but nonetheless treats them with occasional irreverence. For example, Dora's literary mentor, Irish, sometimes says she is vulgar when she is unmoved by his figures of speech. His description of the California sunshine as "insincere" (WC, 121) perplexes her mightily when she subjects the description to her practical brand of literary criticism: "Did he mean the sunshine didn't really mean it? And, if so, what did *that* mean?" (WC, 121). Although Shakespeare is idolized by the Hazards, living writers have more difficulty gaining recognition, and the response to Irish's death outside Graumann's Chinese, the symbol of Hollywood's approval of its own, is "it's only a writer" (WC, 154). Irish does win a posthumous Pulitzer for his *Hollywood Elegies*, but Dora is not sentimental about selling the signed page proofs when she is short of cash.

Despite Dora's introduction of her word processor, and despite the novel's being clearly a written story, her narrative has the sense of an oral tale. She speaks to the reader directly, as if holding a conversation, and interrupts her tale with phrases such as "No. Wait" and "You'll find out soon enough" (WC, 13). She uses dialect and colloquial speech, as in her forebodings about the reception of the film of *A Midsummer Night's Dream*: "we'd passed that fine line that divides the socko from the flopperoo some time before" (WC, 148). At the end of the novel, she accosts the reader as though she and the reader have met in a pub and she has told her story in the course of a drunken evening. Dora's intimacy with the reader is also established by her references to personal details such as the kind of underwear she prefers, her method of applying makeup, and the Revlon color she uses to match her lips and nails. In Irish's work, such details are symbolic, and when he pens his portrait of Dora after she has left him, they are used to convey her hardness and vulgarity. The Hazards' veneration of Shakespeare's language would not, perhaps, extend to Dora's. However elegant the Bard's language may be, Melchior is speaking someone else's words, whereas Dora is speaking in her own voice and voicing her own critical commentary on the monuments of the past.

Reproduction

Carter frequently uses theater imagery in her novels, often as a way of commenting on how identity is constructed on the social stage. For example, the party at the end of *Several Perceptions* is described in the language of staging to point out that in such a context, roles can be changed; Anne Blossom overcomes her limp, Joseph his depression, and Viv his dependency on his mother. The language of the theater signals a liberation from roles the characters may have thought of as fixed. In *Shadow Dance,* this is taken to an extreme by Honeybuzzard, who dresses up and tries to take on different personalities in order to avoid dealing with reality; he can always sidestep a difficult situation by becoming someone else. In *The Magic Toyshop*, Melanie explores her blossoming body by pretending to be figures from art and literature but discovers that such roles are liberating only when she can determine them herself. When Philip tries to impose upon her not only the role of Leda but also the role of passive, subservient womanhood, Melanie finds it frightening. *Nights at the Circus* also explores the duplicity of performing: Fevvers can make an audience contemplate the difficult relation between fact and fiction, but she also needs an audience in order to be herself.

Because *Wise Children* is about a theatrical family, the novel represents all of the venues in which that family performs, including theater, music hall, cinema, and television. The theater in all of its manifestations becomes a metaphor for familial relations, as well as a vehicle for general comments on the culture industry. Presiding over all is the figure of Shakespeare, father of Culture to some in the Hazard dynasty, but to others Lord of Misrule and music hall. Carter called Shakespeare the "intellectual equivalent of bubble-gum," but noted that he is a writer who "can make twelve-year-old girls cry, can foment revolutions in Africa, can be translated into Japanese and leave not a dry eye in the house."[3]

This cheeky, anticanonical stance on Shakespeare translates, in *Wise Children*, into subversive discussions of high and low culture and of the connection between culture and imperialism. Thus, if Shakespeare is seen as the voice of cultural authority, that voice is always in conversation with a number of others. "Shakespeare" is a concept open to myriad productions and reproductions as comedy, tragedy, farce, music hall, parody, and dance. All of these uses of Shakespeare, many of which are part of the plays themselves, set up a dialogue between various perceptions of culture. One might argue that a parody merely draws its audience's attention to the original and therefore does little to undermine its authority, especially when the original is commonly regarded as the genius of English literature. Carter's comments, however, suggest that Shakespeare invites multiple and powerful responses. Although Ranulph Hazard may think of the Bard as a kind of god, *Wise Children* places Shakespeare firmly in the entertainment industry. In order for such parody to be effective, the audience must share certain codes of understanding. If one had no knowledge of Hamlet's soliloquy, "To be, or not to be,"[4] for example, there would be no reference point for the Chance sisters' skit in which they dress as bellhops and ponder whether a package should be delivered to room "2b or not 2b" (*WC*, 90). The parody assumes some familiarity with the original but at the same time points to differences from it. Carter's intertexts are frequently used to create this kind of dialogue, and it is clear that Dora is, as it were, writing back to the voices of the past.

Ranulph has an evangelical zeal when it comes to playing Shakespeare, and his mission is to conquer the world in Shakespeare's name. The success of his traveling company, however, is measured by the number of towns that rename themselves Hazard in his, and more likely his wife's, honor. That his particular brand of Bard-worship is called into question is made clear when Dora listens to a wax cylinder on which Ranulph's voice is recorded: "it was ugly, almost—harsh, grating" (*WC*, 15). His voice makes her shudder because it seems to emanate "from another kind of life entirely" (*WC*, 16). Ranulph's madness is apparent in his inability to distinguish between life and art: he kills his wife, her lover and then himself during a run of *Othello* whose plot spills over the limits of the stage. Melchior's career seems in many ways to repeat his father's. Not only does Melchior, like his father, marry his Cordelia, but at his 100th birthday party, Melchior arrays himself in the costume his father wore as Lear. In directing the film of *A Midsummer Night's Dream*, Melchior exhibits the same grandiosity in bringing Shakespeare's language to the uninitiated, but like Ranulph, Melchior interprets the play too literally, and this proves to be its downfall. The set, for example, makes concrete all the suggestiveness of Shakespeare's language. Nothing is left to the imagination, not even the relationship between the King and Queen of the Fairies, which Melchior, playing Oberon, imitates by having an affair with, and then marrying, Daisy, who plays Titania.

Reproduction in *Wise Children* is a vexed issue in more than the biological sense. Both Ranulph and Melchior use Shakespeare as a colonizing force, as an example of culture that, because of its assumed eternal verity, will easily reproduce itself in another location. In Hollywood, Melchior reproduces an English colony in which tea is served in the afternoon and cricket is played on the lawn. Dora and Nora stay in a Hollywood hotel called the Forest of Arden, and the bust of Shakespeare (in which they have transported sacred soil from England, but has been used by Daisy's cat as a litter box) has been set up in a candlelit alcove by a chambermaid who thinks it is a relic. Like everything else in his career, Melchior's colonial attitude is a spectacle put on for the benefit of the media, although what interests the press is not the movie but the stars and their antics. This, combined with the farcical and excessive nature of Hollywood's version of Shakespeare, mitigates against Melchior's notion that he can reproduce the culture, the language, and the authority of Shakespeare in a different milieu.

Further underlining the failure of this colonial enterprise is the sad story of Gorgeous George, a music hall comedian whose act Dora and Nora see on their 13th birthday. Appropriately, the centerpiece of his program is a joke about a young man who cannot find a wife because each woman he approaches seems to be the result of his father's philandering. When the young man's mother comments on his sad face and he tells her the problem, she tells him to marry whomever he likes because " *'e*'s not your father!" (*WC*, 65). George's finale is a striptease, but an unusual one because tattooed on his body is a map of the world with the British Empire in pink. He is a walking advertisement for colonialism, yet when he is cast as Bottom in Melchior's film, he is a dismal failure because he is out of context. Although his brand of humor is perfectly suited to Bottom's part, he cannot speak the lines without the sort of innuendo that made him popular in Brighton. In Shakespeare's play, Bottom, wearing the head of an ass, is beloved by Titania, whose eyes Oberon has bewitched. When Quince, one of Bottom's fellow mechanicals, sees him wearing this head, Quince says "Thou art translated."[5] Bottom's transformation into, as his friends see it, an ass, is paralleled in *Wise Children*. Gorgeous George does not in fact translate into American culture; rather, his brand of humor makes him into an ass from which his career will never recover. His final appearance in the novel is as a beggar whom Dora meets as she arrives at Melchior's party. She gives him a 20-pound note with Shakespeare's head on it, on the condition that he spend all of it on liquor. In this way, the culture of Shakespeare continues to contribute to George's decline.

Dora's reproduction of her family's story is theatrical in its own right. She frequently reminds the reader that her memory is fading and thereby implicitly raises the question as to how much of her memoir is fact and how much is fiction. Karl Marx's much quoted comment that "all the great events and characters of world history occur, so to speak, twice. . . . the first time as tragedy, the second as farce"[6] seems literally true of Dora's narrative. Although she consciously expunges discussion of tragedies such as the two world wars from her story and puts a comic, even farcical, face on the relations of her family, her narrative still suggests that it is a reproduction of something prior to it. This illusion of realism is undermined by her comments on her mis-remembering events as well as by her theatrical language. Because *Wise Children* draws on Shakespeare's plays, the reader's interpretation of those plays is an important, but not unique, element in creating the family's history. Dora's narrative is full of gaps and omissions, some of which she fills in, some of which she simply notes. Peregrine's adventures as a young boy, for example, are offered as a series of stories, Dora says, so "we could choose which ones we wanted" (*WC*, 31). Grandma Chance is a similar mystery, and her boardinghouse, like so many of the settings in the novel, looks like a stage set. Dora also describes Lynde Court as a stage set, and Melchior's bedroom in Regent's Park as "self-conscious" (*WC*, 219). She compares being accepted by the family that has for so long ignored them to being invited onto the stage. Her narrative thus becomes itself a performance. That she dislikes the set of *A Midsummer Night's Dream* for being too literal suggests that she thinks of her own sets as encouraging imagination and illusion.

The party that ends the novel in chapter 5 has much in common with the confusing excess of the film in chapter 3. Although Hollywood is closed to Melchior after the disaster of this film, he seems to reproduce much of its ethos in his birthday party. The entire affair is captured on celluloid by journalists who barely know where to point their cameras, given the numerous family skeletons that keep popping out of the closets. The entire cast of the novel is reassembled. Those thought dead, Peregrine and Tiffany, are alive; paternity is divulged; and past misdemeanors are revealed. Everything happens at a fever pitch, and when Daisy wonders who holds "the mini-series rights" (*WC*, 216), she captures the tone of the event perfectly. The melodrama, the brimming hearts and eyes, and the staged responses even to spontaneous revelations are all completely over the top. Clearly, media stardom and soap opera have eclipsed stage drama, although Dora is surprised to be reminded by her sister, after one particularly moving revelation, that the curtain did not come down, and that the audience did not rise to its feet. Dora does confess to her reading audience that her tale might be a touch hard to swallow. Were the tale a tragedy, would she need to ask readers to suspend their disbelief?

Dream Vales and Fairy Tales

At the end of the novel, Dora suggests that hers has been an oral tale, told in an informal setting and lubricated by alcohol. Her voice—earthy, colloquial, and practical—narrates the story, but she includes a host of other voices to harmonize with her own. She is, of course, a song-and-dance girl whose success, as she repeats throughout the novel, depends on her being half of a pair with Nora. No single voice, she implies, will be as engaging as a double or even multiple one. Her grandfather's voice is no model because it is harsh and ugly; Melchior's tone is rich, but the words he utters are not his own. While Dora's voice certainly dominates, she invokes a polyphony of other voices because she does not want to deny other speakers, except, perhaps, the old men in the sky who foment war. At the end of the novel, Nora says that she used to wish her father were dead, but this is not Dora's solution to the problem of paternal authority, either literary or biological.

Her strategy is to use parody and multiplicity to question and write back to those fathers, and one of the ways she does so is through *A Midsummer Night's Dream*. The play, together with the 1935 film of it directed by Max Reinhardt, figures largely, although Reinhardt's film both is and is not the one whose production takes place in the novel. The play begins with a statement of paternal authority of the sort that is generally abhorred in Carter's fiction, but such authority is dealt with ironically and specifically in *Wise Children*. When Hermia's father, Egeus, complains that she will not follow his will in her choice of husband, Duke Theseus says, "To you your father should be as a god" (1.1.46). Hermia's response, "I would my father looked but with my eyes" (1.1.56), is met with Theseus's "Rather your eyes must with his judgement look" (1.1.57). The penalty for disobedience is extreme, and Theseus informs Hermia that her choices are "either to die the death, or to abjure / For ever the society of men" (1.1.65–66). Because of this stricture, Hermia and Lysander flee Athens, hoping for sanctuary with Lysander's widowed aunt. They are pursued into the woods by Demetrius, Hermia's intended, and Helena, who dotes on Demetrius. The love potion with which Puck anoints the eyes of the lovers while they sleep leads to both men's pursuing Helena, while abandoning Hermia. But all is set right: the lovers are united, Theseus abandons his strict law, and the play ends with a triple wedding. What happened in the woods now appears to all as if it had been a dream.

Like *Wise Children*, the play reconstructs tragedy in a lighter vein. The extreme nature of Theseus's proposed punishment, however, is only one of several suggestions of violence. Theseus says to his captive bride Hippolyta, "I wooed thee with my sword, / And won thy love doing thee injuries" (1.1.16–17). Love is constructed as a hunt in the forest, too, where the lovers run from and after each other. Even the production of *Pyramus and Thisbe*, the play within the play, is described as a "most lamentable comedy" (1.2.11–12) and, despite its ending with the lovers' deaths, is acted by the mechanicals in a most humorous way. The double perspective of violent or tragic events seen with a comic eye is mirrored by Dora's narration. Because Dora refuses to act in tragedy, she has to revise her tale accordingly, although she never quite succeeds in eliminating the tragedy from the tale, and she criticizes Peregrine for his comment, "Life's a carnival" (*WC*, 222) by suggesting that he listen to the news. As is clear from the eye imagery in both texts, the perspective from which one looks has much to do with what one sees. Dora's illegitimacy gives her an ironic view of the world. She is a child of comedy; the actor and the housemaid, and the music hall and the farce, all contribute to her making. Like Hermia, Dora resists seeing through the eyes of her father's judgment and constructs her story with her own voice and her own perspective on literary paternity.

In Carter's preface to *The Virago Book of Fairy Tales* (1990), she writes about recurring themes in the fairy tale, many of which are apparent in *Wise Children*. Carter edited, translated, and rewrote versions of classic fairy tales, and her interest in them derives from her feminist critique of Western culture and civilization. *The Bloody Chamber* (1979) is her best-known and most often written-about collection, and in most of its tales, she retells fictions of female development in order to focus on female eroticism in a way that she also derives from Sade, whose "work concerns the nature of sexual freedom and is of particular significance to women because of his refusal to see female sexuality in relation to its reproductive function" (*SW*, 1). This is Carter's refusal too, although her methods are seldom the same twice because she explores such myriad ways in which women's sexuality can be expressed. Some of these have caused critics to frown, as when in "The Company of Wolves," for example, Red Riding Hood seduces the wolf who has just devoured her grandmother, or when the heroine's animal sexuality becomes clear in "The Tiger's Bride." Carter's stories have been criticized for not always allowing possibilities of freedom for her female characters, but to provide a single solution would undermine Carter's richly complex vision of the world. As she says of her selection of material for *The Virago Book of Fairy Tales*, "Sisters under the skin we might be, but that doesn't mean we've got much in common. Rather, I wanted to demonstrate the extraordinary richness and diversity of responses to the same human predicament—being alive—and the richness and diversity with which femininity, in practice, is represented in 'unofficial culture.' "[7] This is the editorial policy for this collection, but it is also an appropriate description of the rest of her work. Critics often find Carter hard to place because her writing does not fit neatly into any one genre, any more than her writing proposes any one way of women's dealing with various emanations of patriarchy. It seems thus especially ironic that John Bayley should accuse her of being "politically correct"[8] when her work suggests so many subversive and ingenious ways of dealing with the world.

Wise Children certainly shares some of the characteristics of the fairy tale, and the reason, perhaps, for making *A Midsummer Night's Dream* the centerpiece of the novel is that it is a play about fairies. In her narrative, Dora imitates what Carter describes as fairy tales' "endless recycling process" (*FT*, xi) in putting her story together, and many of Shakespeare's plays provide the material for doing so. Dora's story also partakes of "unofficial" culture in that her story focuses not on the legitimate but on the illegitimate in family, in theater, and also in style. Her colloquial narration and her own references to her story's being an oral tale further place her within the oral tradition in which fairy tales were passed from one generation to the next. Because fairy tales are the products of many different voices, told and retold in many languages with many variations, references to fairy tales add multiple layers to the novel. Although we may commonly use the phrase "fairy tale" to indicate good fortune and happy endings, fairy tales are often brutally violent; they may include elements such as incest, cruelty, mutilation, and death. As Carter describes them, fairy-tale families "are, in the main, dysfunctional units in which parents and step-parents are neglectful to the point of murder and sibling rivalry to the point of murder is the norm" (*FT*, ix). Looked at from this perspective, it becomes clear, once again, how Dora's decision to stick to the comic realm defies her own plot and the precedents of her literary references. Her fairy tale does have a happy ending, but it also suggests just how difficult achieving a happy ending can be. In the Bristol Trilogy, whose settings and style are closer to realism, female characters respond to adversity with masochism. The novels that suggest alternatives to self-immolation, however, are invariably fantastic, implying, perhaps, that these alternatives still happen mostly within the realm of fantasy. Despite their fairy godfather, Peregrine, Dora and Nora make their own way in the world, and their comic vision saves them from despair. The end of the novel gives neither of them a handsome prince, but merely a little bit of affection from a father in a pasteboard crown. However, Peregrine does produce, as if by magic from the pockets of his coat, the twin babies who will give Dora and Nora a stake in the future, and a reason to continue singing and dancing.

Conclusion

Despite—or perhaps because of—her novels' irreverence, quirky humor, and eroticism, Angela Carter has become a central figure in the contemporary British canon. Carter is now one of the most popular British novelists in university curricula, and in the year following her death there were at least 40 proposals for doctoral dissertations on her work in Britain alone.[1] Because her writing is imbued with theoretical and political insights, communicated in lush and extravagant prose, it appeals to a broad spectrum of readers. Her wide range of imagery drawn from literature, film, and philosophy also repays consideration from a variety of perspectives.

To compare Carter's fiction to that of other contemporary writers is not easy. According to Lorna Sage, one of Carter's own heroes was Gabriel García Márquez, whose writing she admired for the ease with which it moved from the everyday to the fantastic. Marquez, writes Sage, "helped Carter's confidence in the continuity you could create between these supposedly disparate ways of describing the world."[2] The group of British postmodern writers with whom I see connections includes Salman Rushdie, Sara Maitland, Julian Barnes, Graham Swift, Jeannette Winterson, Alasdair Gray, and Peter Ackroyd. Carter also shares interest in the Gothic and the romance with writers such as Fay Weldon, Marina Warner, Maggie Gee, and Emma Tennant, among others. To say Carter is "like" any of these novelists, however, is to stretch a point. Insofar as all of these writers are concerned with changing the parameters of fiction by challenging readers' preconceptions about literary form and story, and even about language itself, these writers share a good deal. How each one achieves those ends, though, is remarkably and excitingly different.

Carter risks portraying complexities, particularly with regard to her female characters, and while this approach causes both outrage and adulation, it never leads to indifference. In both fiction and nonfiction, she is provocative, outspoken, and wickedly observant. She remarked that in writing book reviews she was "conscientiously blue-pencilling out her first gut reactions—'bloody awful,' 'fucking dire'—in order to give a more balanced and objective overview."[3] Expletives may be deleted from her writing in fact, but they remain in spirit. Her nonfiction essays provoke outright laughter through no more than a pointed turn of phrase. She has a keen eye for detail and a sharp pen for pretension.

Salman Rushdie's comment that Carter's novels "are like nobody else's"[4] is as acute an observation as one could make about her work. Despite references in her work to a great many different writers, Carter's own writing is never derivative. It speaks for itself in a highly original and completely engaging voice.

Notes and References

Preface

1. Angela Carter, *Expletives Deleted: Selected Writings* (London: Chatto and Windus, 1992), 1.
2. Lorna Sage, ed., *Flesh and the Mirror: Essays on the Art of Angela Carter* (London: Virago, 1994), 1; hereafter cited as Sage, *Flesh and the Mirror*.
3. Ibid., 3.
4. Salman Rushdie, introduction to *Burning Your Boats: Stories*, by Angela Carter (London: Chatto and Windus, 1995), ix.

Chapter One

1. Angela Carter, "Notes from the Front Line," in *On Gender and Writing*, ed. Michelene Wandor (London: Pandora Press, 1983), 73.
2. Susannah Clapp, introduction to *The Curious Room: Plays, Film Scripts and an Opera*, by Angela Carter, ed. Mark Bell (London: Chatto and Windus, 1996), ix.
3. Carmen Callil, "Flying Jewelry," *Sunday Times*, 23 February 1992, sec. 7, p. 6.
4. Lorna Sage, *Angela Carter* (London: Northcote House, 1994), 1; hereafter cited in text as Sage, *Angela Carter*.
5. Robert Coover, "A Passionate Remembrance," *Review of Contemporary Fiction* 14, no. 3 (1994): 9.
6. Callil, "Flying Jewelry," sec. 7, p. 6.
7. Rushdie, introduction to *Burning Your Boats*, ix.
8. Coover, "A Passionate Remembrance," 9.
9. Angela Carter, *Nothing Sacred: Selected Writings* (London: Virago Press, 1982; rev. ed., 1992), 28; hereafter cited in text as *NS*.
10. Angela Carter, "Sugar Daddy," in *Fathers: Reflections by Daughters*, ed. Ursula Owen (London: Virago Press, 1983), 9.
11. Ibid., 7.
12. Callil, "Flying Jewelry," sec. 7, p. 6.
13. Scott Bradfield, "Remembering Angela Carter ," *Review of Contemporary Fiction* 14, no. 3 (1994): 93.
14. Carter, *Expletives Deleted*, 2.
15. Coover, "A Passionate Remembrance," 9.
16. Susannah Clapp, introduction to *American Ghosts and Old World Wonders,* by Angela Carter (London: Chatto and Windus, 1993), ix.

Chapter Two

1. Margaret Atwood, "A Rich Dessert from a Saucy Carter," review of *Burning Your Boats*, by Angela Carter, *(Toronto) Globe and Mail*, 6 April 1996, C18.
2. Ibid.
3. Angela Carter, *The Sadeian Woman: An Exercise in Cultural History* (London: Virago Press, 1979), 1; hereafter cited in text as *SW*.
4. A. Sebestyn, "The Mannerist Marketplace," *New Socialist*, March 1987, 38.
5. John Bayley, "Fighting for the Crown," *The New York Review of Books*, 23 April 1992, 9.
6. Hermione Lee, "A Room of One's Own or a Bloody Chamber?" in Sage, *Flesh and the Mirror,* 308–20.
7. Linda Hutcheon, *A Poetics of Postmodernism: History, Theory, Fiction* (London and New York: Routledge, 1988), ix.
8. Ibid., 23.
9. Angela Carter, *Come unto these Yellow Sands* (Newcastle upon Tyne: Bloodaxe Books Ltd., 1985), 7.
10. Angela Carter, "Ashputtle or The Mother's Ghost: Three Versions of One Story," in *Burning Your Boats*, 390; hereafter cited in text as "A."
11. Angela Carter, *The Passion of New Eve* (London: Virago Press, 1982), 47.

Chapter Three

1. Angela Carter, "Truly, It Felt Like Year One," in *Very Heaven: Looking Back at the Sixties*, ed. Sara Maitland (London: Virago, 1988), 215; hereafter cited in text as "Year One."
2. Marc O'Day labels these novels collectively "The Bristol Trilogy" for the city in which Carter was living when she wrote them, as well as for "the formal and thematic elements they share," in " 'Mutability is Having a Field Day': The Sixties Aura of Angela Carter's Bristol Trilogy," in Sage, *Flesh and the Mirror,* 25.
3. Burgess's comment is reproduced on the dust jacket of the first edition of *Shadow Dance*.
4. There are two lengthy critical commentaries on *Shadow Dance*: O'Day, "Carter's Bristol Trilogy," in Sage, *Flesh and the Mirror,* 25–40; Sage, *Angela Carter,* 9–15).
5. Review of *Honeybuzzard*, by Angela Carter, *New Yorker*, 4 March 1967, 163.
6. John Bowen, "Grotesques," review of *Honeybuzzard*, by Angela Carter, *New York Times Book Review*, 19 February 1967, 44.
7. Angela Carter, "Notes from the Front Line," in *On Gender and Writing*, ed. Michelene Wandor (London: Pandora Press, 1983), 70; hereafter cited in text as "Notes."

8.   Angela Carter, *Shadow Dance* (London: Heinemann, 1966), 23–24; hereafter cited in text as *SD*.

9.   Julia Kristeva, "Word, Dialogue and Novel," in *The Kristeva Reader*, ed. Toril Moi (Oxford: Basil Blackwell, 1986), 37.

10.   Jonathan Swift, *Gulliver's Travels*, ed. Peter Dixon and John Chalker (Harmondsworth: Penguin, 1967), 257–60.

11.   John Haffenden, "Angela Carter," *Novelists in Interview* (London: Methuen, 1985), 86.

12.   Angela Carter, "The Alchemy of the Word," in *Expletives Deleted: Selected Writings* (London: Chatto & Windus, 1992), 73; hereafter cited in text as "Alchemy."

13.   The name "Ghislaine" is a feminization of Ghislain (a.k.a. Gislenus), a saint and Frankish recluse who died in 680. (The Benedictine Monks of St. Augustine's Abbey, Ramsgate, *The Book of Saints* (London: A. C. Black, 1989). The *Middle English Dictionary* (ed. Sherman M. Kuhn and John Reidy [Ann Arbor: University of Michigan Press, 1963]) cites "gislen" (late O.E.) as meaning "to give as a hostage," which seems metaphorically appropriate for Ghislaine's plight. Carter read Medieval English at Bristol University, but whether these references are "intentional" is anybody's guess.

14.   Anna Katsavos, "An Interview with Angela Carter," *Review of Contemporary Fiction* 14, no. 3 (1994): 12.

15.   Angela Carter, *Several Perceptions* (London: Heinemann, 1968), 11; hereafter cited in text as *SP*.

16.   O'Day, "Carter's Bristol Trilogy," 41.

17.   Ibid., 46.

18.   Richard Boston, "Logic in a Schizophrenic's World," review of *Several Perceptions*, by Angela Carter, *New York Times Book Review*, 2 March 1969, 42.

19.   O'Day, "Carter's Bristol Trilogy," 41.

20.   Boston, "Logic," 42.

21.   Mikhail Bakhtin, *Rabelais and His World*, trans. Hélène Iswolsky (Bloomington: Indiana University Press, 1984), 10.

22.   Ibid., 9.

23.   Lorna Sage, "Angela Carter Interviewed by Lorna Sage," in *New Writing*, ed. Malcolm Bradbury and Judy Cook (London: Minerva Press, 1992), 188.

24.   Lorna Sage, *Women in the House of Fiction* (Basingstoke: Macmillan, 1992), 171.

25.   Angela Carter, *Love* (London: Picador, 1988), 3–4; hereafter cited in text as *Love*. *Love* was first published in 1971 by Rupert Hart-Davis, and in a revised edition by Chatto and Windus in 1987. I have chosen to use the Picador edition (a reprint of the revised edition) because it is the most widely available. Lorna Sage, in *Women in the House of Fiction*, discusses some of the changes Carter made in the revised edition.

26. Angela Carter, *Fireworks: Nine Stories in Various Disguises* (New York: Harper and Row, 1981), 133; hereafter cited in text as *FW*.

27. Edgar Allan Poe, "Annabel Lee," in *Selected Writings of Edgar Allan Poe*, ed. Edward H. Davidson (Boston: The Riverside Press, 1956), 46.

28. Michelle A. Massé, *In the Name of Love: Women, Masochism, and the Gothic* (Ithaca and London: Cornell University Press, 1992), 49.

Chapter Four

1. Angela Carter, *Heroes and Villains* (London: Penguin Books, 1988), 124; hereafter cited in text as *HV*.

2. Rosemary Jackson, *Fantasy: The Literature of Subversion* (London: Methuen, 1981), 3.

3. Angela Carter, *The Magic Toyshop* (London: Virago Press, 1981), 152; hereafter cited in text as *MT*.

4. In "The Wound in the Face," from Carter's nonfiction collection *Nothing Sacred* (1982), she writes about the iconography of women's face painting: "To do up your eyes so that they look like self-inflicted wounds is to wear on your face the evidence of the violence your environment inflicts on you" (93–94); "We are so used to the bright red mouth we no longer see it as the wound it mimics, except in the treacherous lucidity of paranoia" (94). In masking herself with her mother's black and red makeup, Melanie seems to be underscoring this point. Because she feels that she has attempted to usurp her mother's sexual power, she makes the wound more evident by smearing the colors all over her face.

5. *The Magic Toyshop* was made into a film by Stephen Morrison in 1988. For a discussion, see Lorna Mulvey, "Cinema Magic and the Old Monsters: Angela Carter's Cinema," in Sage, *Flesh and the Mirror*, 230–42.

6. Angela Carter, "The Loves of Lady Purple," in *Fireworks: Nine Stories in Various Disguises* (New York: Harper and Row, 1974), 24.

7. Paulina Palmer, "From 'Coded Mannequin' to Bird Woman: Angela Carter's Magic Flight," in *Women Reading Women's Writing*, ed. Sue Roe (Brighton, Sussex: Harvester Press, 1987), 180.

8. Sage, *Angela Carter*, 16.

9. Haffenden, "Angela Carter," 95.

10. Robert Clark, "Angela Carter's Desire Machine," *Women's Studies* 14, no.2 (1987): 151.

11. Ibid., 152.

12. Sigmund Freud, "Some Psychical Consequences of the Anatomical Distinction between the Sexes," in *The Pelican Freud Library*, trans. James Strachey, ed. Angela Richards (Harmondsworth: Penguin [1925], 1977) vol. 7, 331–43. "When a little boy first catches sight of a girl's genital region, he begins by showing irresolution and lack of interest. . . . It is not until later, when some threat of castration has obtained a hold upon him, that the observa-

tion becomes important to him: if he then recollects or repeats it, it arouses a terrible storm of emotion in him and forces him to believe in the reality of the threat which he has hitherto laughed at" (336).

13.   Barbara Creed, *The Monstrous Feminine: Film, Feminism, Psychoanalysis* (London: Routledge, 1993), 111.

Chapter Five

1.   Sage, *Angela Carter,* 34.

2.   Angela Carter, *The Infernal Desire Machines of Doctor Hoffman* (Harmondsworth: Penguin, 1985), 206; hereafter cited in text as *IDM.*

3.   Brian McHale, *Postmodernist Fiction* (London and New York: Methuen, 1987), 144.

4.   Ferdinand de Saussure, *Course in General Linguistics*, trans. Roy Harris, ed. Charles Bally and Albert Sechehaye (La Salle, Ill.: Open Court Publishing, 1986), 65–98.

5.   Sigmund Freud, "Beyond the Pleasure Principle," in *The Freud Reader*, ed. Peter Gay (New York: W. W. Norton, 1989), 612.

6.   Ibid., 612.

7.   Peter Brooks, *Reading for the Plot: Design and Intention in Narrative* (Cambridge, Mass.: Harvard University Press, 1992), 112.

8.   Ibid., 112.

9.   René Descartes, *Discourse on Method*, trans. F. E. Sutcliffe (Harmondsworth: Penguin, 1968), 53–54.

10.   Brooks, *Reading*, 103.

11.   Patricia Waugh, *Feminine Fictions: Revisiting the Postmodern* (London and New York: Routledge, 1989), 2.

12.   Linda Hutcheon, *The Politics of Postmodernism* (London and New York: Routledge, 1989), 154.

Chapter Six

1.   Elaine Jordan, "The Dangerous Edge," in Sage, *Flesh and the Mirror*, 213.

2.   Angela Carter, *The Passion of New Eve* (London: Virago Press, 1991), 6; hereafter cited in text as *NE.*

3.   Sage, *Angela Carter,* 34.

4.   Haffenden, "Angela Carter," 87.

5.   Susan Rubin Suleiman, *Subversive Intent: Gender, Politics and the Avant Garde* (Cambridge, Mass., and London: Harvard University Press, 1990), 137.

6.   Teresa de Lauretis, *Alice Doesn't: Feminism, Semiotics, Cinema* (Bloomington: Indiana University Press, 1984), 139.

7.   Ibid., 67–68.

8. Ibid., 69.

9. Joseph Anderson and Barbara Anderson, "Motion Perception in Motion Pictures," in *The Cinematic Apparatus*, ed. Teresa de Lauretis and Stephen Heath (London and Basingstoke: Macmillan, 1980), 85.

10. Ibid., 79.

11. Susan J. Lederman and Bill Nichols, "Flicker and Motion in Film," in *Ideology and the Image: Social Representation in Cinema and Other Media*, ed. Bill Nichols (Bloomington: Indiana University Press, 1981), 299.

12. Judith Butler, *Gender Trouble: Feminism and the Subversion of Identity* (New York and London: Routledge, 1990), 133.

13. Mary Ann Doane, *Femmes Fatales: Feminism, Film Theory, Psychoanalysis* (New York and London: Routledge, 1991), 1.

14. Judith Butler, *Gender Trouble*, 138.

Chapter Seven

1. Rushdie, introduction to *Burning Your Boats*, x.

2. Angela Carter, *Nights at the Circus* (London: Pan Books, 1985), 7; hereafter cited in text as *NC*.

3. Haffenden, "Angela Carter," 88.

4. Ibid., 88.

5. Roland Barthes, *The Pleasure of the Text*, trans. Richard Miller (New York: Farrar, Straus and Giroux, 1975), 9.

6. Roland Barthes, "From Work to Text," in *Image-Music-Text*, trans. Stephen Heath (New York: Hill and Wang, 1971), 163.

7. Michel Foucault, *Discipline and Punish: The Birth of the Prison*, trans. Alan Sheridan (New York: Vintage Books, 1979), 200.

8. N. Katherine Hayles, *Chaos Bound: Orderly Disorder in Contemporary Literature and Science* (Ithaca and London: Cornell University Press, 1990), 265.

9. Ibid., 265.

10. Paul Davies, *The Cosmic Blueprint: New Discoveries in Nature's Creative Ability to Order the Universe* (New York: Simon and Schuster, 1988), 14.

11. N. Katherine Hayles, ed., *Chaos and Order: Complex Dynamics in Literature and Science* (Chicago and London: Chicago University Press, 1991), 10–11.

12. Hayles, *Chaos Bound*, 147.

13. Joanne M. Gass, "Panopticism in *Nights at the Circus*," *Review of Contemporary Fiction* 14, no. 3 (1994): 75.

14. Haffenden, "Angela Carter," 88.

15. Ibid., 88.

16. Victor Turner, *The Ritual Process: Structure and Anti-Structure* (Ithaca: Cornell University Press, 1977), 94.

17. Sage, "Angela Carter Interviewed," 190.

18. Terry Caesar, "Motherhood and Postmodernism," *American Literary History* 7, no. 1 (1995): 129.

Chapter Eight

1. Angela Carter, *Wise Children* (London: Chatto and Windus, 1991), 153; hereafter cited in text as *WC*.
2. Salman Rushdie, "Angela Carter, 1940–1992: A Very Good Wizard, a Very Dear Friend," *New York Times Book Review*, 8 March 1992, 5.
3. Sage, "Angela Carter Interviewed," 186.
4. William Shakespeare, *Hamlet Prince of Denmark* (Harmondsworth: Penguin, 1985), 3.1.52.
5. William Shakespeare, *A Midsummer Night's Dream* (Harmondsworth: Penguin, 1983), 3.1.107; hereafter cited in text by act, scene, and line reference.
6. Karl Marx, "The Eighteenth Brumaire of Louis Napoleon," in *Surveys from Exile: Political Writings*, vol. 2 (Harmondsworth: Penguin, 1992), 146.
7. Angela Carter, ed., *The Virago Book of Fairy Tales* (London: Virago, 1990), xiv; hereafter cited in text as *FT*.
8. Bayley, "Fighting for the Crown," 9.

Conclusion

1. Peter Parker, ed., "Angela Carter," in *The Reader's Companion to Twentieth-Century Writers* (Oxford: Helicon Publishing Ltd., 1995), 134.
2. Sage, *Flesh and the Mirror,* 1–2.
3. Carter, introduction to *Expletives Deleted*, 1.
4. Rushdie, introduction to *Burning Your Boats*, ix.

Selected Bibliography

PRIMARY WORKS

Novels

Shadow Dance. London: Heinemann, 1966; reprinted as *Honeybuzzard*, New York: Simon & Schuster, 1966; London: Pan, 1968.

The Magic Toyshop. London: Heinemann, 1967; New York: Simon & Schuster, 1968; London: Virago, 1981.

Several Perceptions. London: Heinemann, 1968; New York: Simon & Schuster, 1968; London: Virago, 1981; London: Virago, 1995.

Heroes and Villains. London: Heinemann, 1968; New York: Simon & Schuster, 1969; London: Pan, 1970.

Love. London: Rupert Hart-Davis, 1971; rev. ed., London: Chatto & Windus, 1987; New York: Viking Penguin, 1988; London: Picador, 1988.

The Infernal Desire Machines of Doctor Hoffman. London: Rupert Hart-Davis, 1972; reprinted as *The War of Dreams*, New York: Bard/Avon Books, 1977; Harmondsworth: Penguin, 1982.

The Passion of New Eve. London: Gollancz, 1977; New York: Harcourt, Brace Jovanovich, 1977; London: Virago, 1982.

Nights at the Circus. London: Chatto & Windus, 1984; New York: Viking, 1985; London: Pan, 1985.

Wise Children. London: Chatto and Windus, 1991; New York: Farrar, Straus and Giroux, 1992; London: Vintage, 1992.

Short-Story Collections

Fireworks: Nine Profane Pieces. London: Quartet Books, 1974; New York: Harper & Row, 1981; rev. ed., London: Chatto & Windus, 1987; London: Virago, 1988.

The Bloody Chamber and Other Stories. London: Gollancz, 1979; New York: Harper & Row, 1980; Harmondsworth: Penguin, 1981.

Black Venus. London: Chatto & Windus, 1985; reprinted as *Saints and Strangers*, New York: Viking Penguin, 1987; London: Pan, 1986.

American Ghosts and Old World Wonders. London: Chatto & Windus, 1993; London: Vintage, 1994.

Burning Your Boats: Stories. London: Chatto & Windus, 1995.

The Curious Room: Plays, Film Scripts and an Opera. London: Chatto and Windus, 1996.

Nonfiction

The Sadeian Woman: An Exercise in Cultural History. London: Virago, 1979;
    reprinted as *The Sadeian Woman and the Ideology of Pornography*, New
    York: Pantheon, 1979.
Translator and Foreword. *The Fairy Tales of Charles Perrault*. London: Gollancz,
    1977; New York: Bard Books, 1979.
"The Language of Sisterhood." In *The State of the Language*, edited by Leonard
    Michaels and Christopher Ricks. Berkeley: University of California Press,
    1980.
Nothing Sacred: Selected Writings. London: Virago, 1982; rev. ed., London:
    Virago, 1992.
Editor and translator. *Sleeping Beauty and Other Favourite Fairy Tales*. London:
    Gollancz, 1982; New York: Schoken, 1989; London: Gollancz, 1991.
"Notes from the Front Line." In *On Gender and Writing*, edited by Michelene
    Wandor. London: Pandora Press, 1983.
"Sugar Daddy." In *Fathers: Reflections by Daughters*, edited by Ursula Owen.
    London: Virago Press, 1983.
Editor. *Wayward Girls and Wicked Women*. London: Virago, 1986; London: Pen-
    guin, 1989.
Images of Frida Kahlo. London: Redstone Press, 1989.
Editor. *The Virago Book of Fairy Tales*. London: Virago, 1990; reprinted as *Old Wives'
    Fairy Tale Book*. New York: David McKay, 1987; London: Virago, 1991.
Expletives Deleted: Selected Writings. London: Chatto & Windus, 1992; Vintage,
    1993.
Editor. *The Second Virago Book of Fairy Tales*. London: Virago, 1992; London:
    Virago, 1993.

Radio Plays

Come unto these Yellow Sands: Four Radio Plays. Newcastle on Tyne: Bloodaxe
    Books, 1985; Dufour Editions, 1985.

Children's Books

Miss Z, The Dark Young Lady. London: Heinemann, 1970; New York: Simon
    and Schuster, 1970.
The Donkey Prince. New York: Simon and Schuster, 1970.
Martin Leman's Comic and Curious Cats. London: Gollancz, 1979; Gollancz, 1988.
Moonshadow. London: Gollancz, 1982.

Poetry

Unicorn. Leeds: Location Press, 1966.

SECONDARY WORKS

Books, Parts of Books, and Collections

Bradbury, Malcolm. *The Modern British Novel.* London: Secker and Warburg, 1993. Puts Carter in the context of contemporary British women's writing.

Britzolakis, Christina. "Angela Carter's Fetishism." *Textual Practice* 9, no. 3 (1995): 459–76. Excellent essay on femininity as spectacle. Particularly good on *Love.*

Ferrell, Robyn. "Life-Threatening Life: Angela Carter and the Uncanny." In *The Illusion of Life: Essays on Animation*, edited by Alan Cholodenko. Sydney: Power Publications; Australian Film Commission, 1991. Feminist analysis of Freud's "Uncanny" with regard to *The Magic Toyshop.*

Gasiorek, Andrzej. *Post-War British Fiction: Realism and After.* London: Edward Arnold, 1995. Discusses Carter's political strategies in narrative. Interesting analysis of Doctor Hoffman from the perspective of Plato's *Republic.*

Gass, Joanne M., ed. *Angela Carter. The Review of Contemporary Fiction* 14, no. 3 (1994). A useful collection of sophisticated articles. Includes two interviews with Carter.

Hutcheon, Linda. *The Politics of Postmodernism.* London and New York: Routledge, 1989. Discussion of desire and eroticism in "Black Venus."

Jordan, Elaine. "Enthralment: Angela Carter's Speculative Fictions." In *Plotting Change: Contemporary Women's Fiction*, edited by Linda Anderson. London: Edward Arnold, 1990. Discusses Carter's political sense and argues against Robert Clark's speculation that Carter writes in the service of patriarchy.

———. "The Dangers of Angela Carter." In *New Feminist Discourses: Critical Essays on Theories and Texts*, edited by Isobel Armstrong. London and New York: Routledge, 1992.

Kendrick, Walter. "The Real Magic of Angela Carter." In *Contemporary British Women Writers*, edited by Robert E. Hosmer Jr. New York: St. Martin's Press, 1993. A general survey that raises interesting points about Carter's subversive imagination with regard to female sexuality.

Landon, Brooks. "Eve at the End of the World: Sexuality and the Reversal of Expectations in Novels by Joanna Russ, Angela Carter, and Thomas Berger." In *Erotic Universe: Sexuality and Fantastic Literature*, edited by Donald Palumbo. New York: Greenwood, 1986. Brief, insightful comments on sexual stereotypes and mythology in *Heroes and Villains.*

Lathers, Marie. "Fin-de-siecle Eves in Villiers de l'Isle-Adam and Angela Carter." In *Literature and the Bible*, edited by David Bevan. Amsterdam: Rodopi, 1993. *The Passion of New Eve* from the perspective of its rewritten Edens and late-twentieth-century interest in reproductive technology, race, and gender.

Lewallen, Avis. "Wayward Girls but Wicked Women? Female Sexuality in Angela Carter's *The Bloody Chamber.*" In *Perspectives on Pornography: Sexuality in Film and Literature*, edited by Gary Day and Clive Bloom. New York: St. Martin's, 1988. *The Bloody Chamber* read through *The Sadeian Woman.*

Meaney, Gerardine. *(Un)like Subjects: Women, Theory, Fiction*. London and New York: Routledge, 1993. Analyses of *Heroes and Villains*, *The Sadeian Woman*, and *Wise Children* in the light of contemporary feminist theory.

Palmer, Paulina. "From 'Coded Mannequin' to Bird Woman: Angela Carter's Magic Flight." In *Women Reading Women's Writing*, edited by Sue Roe. Brighton: Harvester Press, 1987. Discussion of the changing characterization of female characters in Carter's novels.

Punter, David. "Essential Imaginings: The Novels of Angela Carter and Russell Hoban." In *The British and Irish Novel since 1960*, edited by James Acheson. New York: St. Martin's, 1991. Carter in the context of magic realism, appropriately defined as seeing the world through transformed eyes.

———. *The Literature of Terror: A History of Gothic Fictions from 1765 to the Present Day*. London: Longman, 1980. Discussion of the Gothic elements in *Heroes and Villains*.

Robinson, Sally. *Engendering the Subject: Gender and Self-Representation in Contemporary Women's Fiction*. Albany: State University of New York Press, 1991.

Rose, Ellen Cronan. "Through the Looking Glass: When Women Tell Fairy Tales." In *The Voyage In: Fictions of Female Development*, edited by Elizabeth Abel, Marianne Hirsch, and Elizabeth Langland. Hanover, N.H.: University Press of New England, 1983. Analysis of *The Bloody Chamber* in terms of its changing focus from women under patriarchy to relations between mothers and daughters.

Rosinsky, Natalie M. *Feminist Futures: Contemporary Women's Speculative Fiction*. Ann Arbor, Michigan: UMI Research Press, 1982. Focused feminist analysis of the twists and turns of *The Passion of New Eve*.

Russo, Mary. *The Female Grotesque: Risk, Excess and Modernity*. New York and London: Routledge, 1994. Includes a chapter on the grotesque body in *Nights at the Circus*.

Sage, Lorna. "Angela Carter." In *British Novelists since 1960*, edited by Jay L. Halio. Vol. 14 of *The Dictionary of Literary Biography*. Detroit: Gale Research, 1983. A dated but excellent survey.

———. *Angela Carter*. Plymouth: Northcote House, 1994. An appreciation of Carter's life and work by a good friend. On the premise that one cannot separate the writer from the woman, Sage discusses the fiction in light of biographical details. Includes an excellent bibliography, particularly of Carter's uncollected journalism and of critical articles and reviews.

————, ed. *Flesh and the Mirror: Essays on the Art of Angela Carter*. London: Virago, 1994. A collection of essays on various aspects of Carter's work including science fiction, cinema, surrealism, and fairy tales.

————. *Women in the House of Fiction*. Basingstoke: Macmillan, 1992. Good introduction to Carter's work. Includes discussion of the differences between the two editions of *Love*.

Segal, David, ed. "Angela Carter." In *Short Story Criticism*. Vol. 13. Detroit: Gale Research, 1993. Providing excerpts from articles written about Carter's short fiction, this is an invaluable research tool.

Steedman, Carolyn. "New Time: Mignon and Her Meanings." In *Fin de Siecle/Fin du Globe: Fears and Fantasies of the Late Nineteenth Century*, edited by John Stokes. New York: St. Martin's, 1992. A clever essay on the reshaping of "Mignon" from Goethe through Freud to *Nights at the Circus*.

Suleiman, Susan Rubin. *Subversive Intent: Gender, Politics, and the Avant-Garde*. Cambridge, Mass., and London: Harvard University Press, 1990. Insightful discussion of *The Passion of New Eve* as an example of feminist writing practice.

Warner, Marina. *From the Beast to the Blonde: Fairy Tales and Their Tellers*. London: Vintage, 1995. Several references to Carter's fairy tales and fairy-tale motifs.

Articles

Bryant, Sylvia. "Re-Constructing Oedipus through 'Beauty and the Beast.' " *Criticism* 31, no.4 (1989): 439–53. Interesting comments on the myth of Oedipus in Carter's fairy tales.

Clark, Robert. "Angela Carter's Desire Machine." *Women's Studies* 14, no. 2 (1987): 147–61. A not very careful reading of Carter in which Clark argues that she reinstates patriarchal values.

Collick, John. "Wolves through the Window: Writing Dreams/Dreaming Films/Filming Dreams." *Critical Survey* 3, no. 3 (1991): 283–89. Brief reference to dream imagery in the film of "The Company of Wolves."

Duncker, Patricia. "Re-Imagining the Fairy Tales: Angela Carter's Bloody Chambers." *Literature and History* 10, no. 1 (1984): 3–14. Reads *The Bloody Chamber* through *The Sadeian Woman* and quibbles with the notion of the moral pornographer.

Fowl, Melinda G. "Angela Carter's *The Bloody Chamber* Revisited." *Critical Survey* 3, no. 1 (1991): 71–79. On the motif of the stranger or "other" in the collection.

Lokke, Kari E. "*Bluebeard* and *The Bloody Chamber*: The Grotesque of Self-Parody and Self-Assertion." *Frontiers* 10, no. 1 (1988): 7–12. Compares Carter's Bluebeard to Max Frisch's and argues that the grotesque is a vehicle for exposing patriarchal attitudes.

Matus, Jill. "Blond, Black and Hottentot Venus: Context and Critique in Angela Carter's 'Black Venus.' " *Studies in Short Fiction* 28, no. 4 (1991): 467–76. Looks at Carter's use of historical context in *Black Venus*.

Punter, David. "Angela Carter: Supersessions of the Masculine." *Critique* 25, no. 4 (1984): 209–22. Good analysis of desire, the unconscious, and sexuality in *The Passion of New Eve* and *The Infernal Desire Machines*.

Rubenstein, Roberta. "Intersexions: Gender Metamorphosis in Angela Carter's *The Passion of New Eve*." *Tulsa Studies in Women's Literature* 12, no. 1 (1993): 103–18. Investigates *The Passion of New Eve*'s examination of gender but concludes that the novel remains trapped in a paradigm of dominance and submission.

Schmidt, Ricarda. "The Journey of the Subject in Angela Carter's Fiction." *Textual Practice* 3, no. 1 (1989): 56–75. One of the most quoted essays on Carter details changing cultural ideas about the subject: desire in *The Infernal Desire Machines*; gender in *The Passion of New Eve*; free womanhood in *Nights at the Circus*.

Siegel, Carol. "Postmodern Women Novelists Review Victorian Male Masochism." *Genders* no. 11 (1991): 1–16. Insightful and original essay on male masochism in *Nights at the Circus* and *The Passion of New Eve*.

Turner, Rory, P. B. "Subjects and Symbols: Transformations of Identity in *Nights at the Circus*." *Folklore Forum* 20, nos. 1–2 (1987): 39–60. Particularly useful on the novel's symbols of the carnival and the limen.

Wilson, Robert Rawdon. "SLIP PAGE: Angela Carter, In/Out/In the Postmodern Nexus." *Ariel* 20, no. 4 (1989): 96–114. An essay on postmodernism that makes reference to "Lady of the House of Love" as an example of intersecting discourses.

Vallorani, Nicoletta. "The Body of the City: Angela Carter's *The Passion of New Eve*." *Science Fiction Studies* 21, no. 3 (1994): 365–79. Discusses the representation of utopian cities in feminist science fiction and the connection between the physical and urban body.

Index

The Author

Alison Lee is assistant professor of English at the University of Western Ontario, London, Canada. She has published *Realism and Power: Postmodern British Fiction* (1990), and her academic interests include women's writing, feminist theory, and postmodernism.

The Editor

Kinley E. Roby is professor of English at Northeastern University. He is the Twentieth-Century Field Editor of the Twayne English Authors Series, Series Editor of Twayne's Critical History of British Drama, and General Editor of Twayne's Women and Literature Series. He has written books on Arnold Bennett, Edward VII, and Joyce Cary and edited a collection of essays on T. S. Eliot. He makes his home in Sudbury, Massachusetts.